A HANDBOOK OF ANCIENT WESTERN PHILOSOPHY

A HANDBOOK OF ANCIENT WESTERN PHILOSOPHY

Godfrey O. Ozumba & Michael Ukah

UNIVERSITY OF CALABAR

3RD LOGIC OPTION PUBLISHING
A wholly owned subsidiary of 3rd Logic Option Ltd.
London . Calabar

To all my students in over thirty years teaching career
---- Godfrey O. Ozumba

To all my teachers through-out the years of my study
---- Michael Ukah

3ᴿᴰ LOGIC OPTION PUBLISHING
A wholly owned subsidiary of 3ʳᵈ Logic Option Ltd.
London and Calabar.
www.3rdlogicoption.com
3rdloption@gmail.com

© 2014 by 3ʳᵈ Logic Option Publishing

All rights reserved. No part of this book may be reproduced or utilized in any form or by any means, electronic or mechanical, including photocopying and recording, or by any information storage and retrieval system, without permission in writing from the publisher.

NATIONAL LIBRARY OF NIGERIA CATALOGUING-IN-PUBLICATION DATA

OZUMBA, Godfrey O.

A Handbook of Ancient Western Philosophy.

1. Philosophy, ancient – Handbooks, manuals, history, etc. I. UKAH Michael II. Title.

Includes bibliographical references and index

B 111.O99   2014   100

ISBN: 978-978-52850-0-0 (pbk)

ISBN: 978-978-52850-1-7 (e-bk)   AACR2

The referencing style adopted for this work is the new Calabar School of Philosophy Style Guide. Download manual at www.csp.unical.edu.ng

Printed in UK on *acid –free* paper

TABLE OF CONTENTS

ACKNOWLEDGEMENTS vii

PREFACE viii-ix

FOREWORD x-xi

CHAPTER 1: The Age of Mythology   1-7

CHAPTER 2: Thales of Miletus   8-12

CHAPTER 3: Anaximander of Miletus   13-18

CHAPTER 4: Anaximenes of Miletus   19-22

CHAPTER 5: Xenophanes of Colophon   23

CHAPTER 6: Heraclitus of Ephesus   24-27

CHAPTER 7: Parmenides of Elea   28-34

CHAPTER 8: The Beginning of Dialectics   35-38

CHAPTER 9: Overview of Ancient Philosophy   39-53

CHAPTER 10: The Sophists   54-66

CHAPTER 11: The Golden Era of Greek Philosophy I–Socrates 67-81

CHAPTER 12: The Golden Era of Greek Philosophy II–Plato 82-87

CHAPTER 13: The Golden Era of Greek Philosophy III–Aristotle 88-114

CHAPTER 14: Philosophy after Aristotle   115-122

RELEVANT LITERATURE   123-125

INDEX   126-128

ACKNOWLEDGEMENTS

We wish to express our appreciation to the Almighty God for the grace to put together this material as a fulfillment to our students who have been looking forward to an official publication of this materials generated over the years in the course of our teaching this course both at the undergraduate and postgraduate levels. Our debt of gratitude will immediately go to all the doyens of history of Western philosophy from whose works we both excerpted and have drawn heavily in the course of this work. Notables are Enoch Stumpf, Frederick Copleston and Bertrand Russell, W. T. Jones and Joseph Owens. Our undergraduate and postgraduate Students over the years spanning our teaching careers are duly acknowledged for subtle impetus and goad they provided to instigate this research. We must discharge our debts to all the lecturers in the Calabar School of Philosophy for providing an encouraging and vibrant agora-type philosophical environment that makes research to thrive in the Calabar School of Philosophy. Remembered here are Professors Alozie, Asouzu, Uduigwomen, ijiomah, Olu-Jacob, Drs. Ene, Ojong, Ochulor, Asira, Akpan, Ikegbu, Egbai, Ogar, Mesembe, Inyang, Ncha, Maduka, Edor and Etta as well as Mr. Udofia.

Singled out for special mention is Dr. Jonathan O. Chimakonam for his resolute determination to give this book special attention by way of thorough proofreading and good packaging through his publishing outfit. We say kudos to him as a hard working academic destined to go places. Our typist is here remembered for a good work done. The last but not the least is our families. G. O. Ozumba specifically appreciates his wife Lily and his children, Ifeoma and Ogechukwu. All our benefactors who have unwittingly been unnamed remain named through the vicarious power of their abiding faith in us. God bless you all.

PREFACE

Doing a book on Ancient Western Philosophy is such a drab job because all you have to do is pore through the works of historians of Western philosophy to recapitulate what may be the accepted information and form that have been handed down over the ages. You worry over some taken-for-granted positions and standards but you have very little bases for any agitation. In most World Universities where Ancient Western Philosophy is taug the popular genre is to regurgitate the history of Greek Philosophy from may be, the pre-philosophical period of the poets—Homer and Hesiod and the classical literature that formed the source of early Greek wisdom and from there move on to the dawn of philosophizing blazed by the Milesian Philosophers, Thales, Anaximander and Anaximenes. These are followed by Xenophanes, Heraclitus, Parmenides, Pythagoras, Zeno, Empedocles, Anaxagoras, the Atomists—Leucippus, Democritus, Epicurus and Lucretius. After this period we have the period known as the Socratic period which is characterized by the philosophical position of the sophists notably Protagoras, Thrasymachus, Prodicus, Hippias and Gorgias. After this, the whole idea of Sophism is treated. It is noteworthy to mention here that most historians of the ancient period group Socrates together with the Sophists but others allow Sophism to belong to a period distinct from the Socratic period. Socratic period is in some cases made to represent what we call the golden era of Greek Philosophy. This period is represented by the worthies of Socrates, Plato and Aristotle. But all historians of that period however agree that whether Socrates is placed in the same period with the Sophists or not, the temperament, Style and teachings of Socrates differed markedly from the teaching of the Sophists. This is in fact, one of the reasons the sophists were so incensed against Socrates and sought to destroy him. What is important however is to mention that from the Sophists philosophical orientation changed from cosmological discussions to anthropological interests. Man and his society became the lure for philosophical engagement.

This book is therefore written on the request of my students who have been desirous to have a book that will be easy to understand which captures in a fairly comprehensive way what those who offer this course in their second year of study in this University are expected to know. We have in the course of research depended heavily on the very lucid account provided by Copleston. Others whose books have been drawn heavily from include Bertrand Russell, Owens ,Lewes, Stumpf, Allen, Cornford, Jaeger Werner, Guthrie, W. T. Jones, Paul Edwards, Brehier, Burnet, Gomperz, and others which we cannot remember. Whatever infelicities and inaccuracies that are identifiable with this work are entirely our fault. However, we have endeavored to present the history of ancient period of Western Philosophy as accurately as possible within the ambit of what is available to us as sources. We have covered the familiar scope of the course reaching as far afield as to include the post Aristotelian period. Also treated are discourses on Epicurus, Stoicism, Cynicism, Skepticism, etc. It is hoped that this work will help students and teachers of the history of ancient Western Philosophy to understand the origination and progression of ideas from the earliest beginning of Western thought to the very complex ramifications of knowledge that have come to characterize Western Philosophy in general. The seed of all that we see as Western Philosophy was sown in the innocent and almost uneventful period of the Ionians. This is why the seed of virtually all preceding developments in science, philosophy, social sciences and law can be traced to those innocent beginnings. This is why we have said that the history of Western philosophy is not an abrupt happenstance but a sequential continuum of ideas though characterized by occasional spasmic effusions called antithesis and synthesis of ideas as responses to preceding positions.

Godfrey O. Ozumba and Michael Ukah
Calabar July, 2014

FOREWORD

Undeniably, the history of Western philosophy is a lively and stimulating field characterized by compelling interconnections between different epochs and varying thoughts. It all began in ancient Greece, in a little but commercially important town of Ionia. This era of Western philosophy, known as the ancient epoch till date, offers a rich and enduring resource for the history of philosophy. Despite the scholarly importance and appeal of this epoch, the paucity of current, relevant, and well-informed works coupled with the complexity of the account of the era have been quite challenging for scholars and students in the field. As a consequence, researchers in this field always have to come to terms with intricate situations of intellectual and material doubts, which inexorably demands greater and painstaking research effort in order to overcome such challenges.

Yet, for all disciplines and specialized fields, there is no question that the benefit of daunting research effort far outweighs its frustrations. It is on this note that I commend the diligence of Professor Godfrey Ozumba, a seasoned scholar in the history of philosophy, bringing to fruition this volume: *A Handbook of Ancient Western Philosophy*. As well-regarded expert in the field, Professor Ozumba's dexterity in the handling of the different segments of the ancient history of Western philosophy is a glaring indication of his mastery of the subject matter. Perhaps, the beauty of the work lies in the fact that the author transcends mere presentation of ancient philosophers and their positions to lace up each discourse with critical extrapolations pointing to possible background, cultural and circumstantial influences and, of course, modern implications of each philosopher's thoughts. This sort of multi-perspective and rigorous presentation is something that almost always makes true philosophical writings remarkable. Not only has Professor Ozumba produced a significant corpus in the history of ancient Western philosophy but the stylistic fashion in which he adapts and transposes the account of ancient era for modern time, makes this volume quite fascinating even to non-students of philosophy. Thus, the reader is never turned off by that familiar archaism or the occasional belch of antiquated tone that unavoidably characterizes most text books in ancient Western philosophy. A combination of depth in scope, content, and analysis as well as a beautiful command and rendering of the English language commend this book to the reading pleasure of all, including non-philosophy majors.

I recall with nostalgia my undergraduate education years in Nigeria in the early 1980s when, as a history student, courses in philosophy such as logic, history of Western Philosophy, social and political thoughts, were all mandatory courses which I was prevailed upon to take. Though I am not quite sure about how broad and integrated the curricula of most universities are at the moment, to state that the undergraduate curriculum produced well-rounded students is, perhaps, an understatement. Thanks to Professor Ozumba, for those who never took courses or read much work on philosophy, this book would probably provide just the sort of fillip required to begin your philosophy education. I submit that discourses on the inaugural genius of the Ionians, the fantastic disquiet which the Eleatics brought with them, the incisive and amazing insights by the Pythagoreans, the revolutions by the Sophists and other pre-Socratics, which brilliantly climaxes at the ice-breaking ideologue of the golden era of Greek philosophy, would make a superb reading not only to the green-horns in philosophy but also to the old-war horses of the discipline. As philosophers would always say: a true lover of wisdom never gets enough philosophy! Whether as professional philosophers, pastime readers or curious thinkers on the evolution of most of the greatest sociological, psychological, physiological, anthropological and scientific ideas that make waves in modern scholarship, a good grounding couched in this Handbook is imperative.

Apollos Okwuchi Nwauwa, PhD
Professor of History & Africana Studies
Director, Africana Studies Program
Bowling Green State University
Bowling Green, Ohio, USA

About the Authors

Godfrey O. Ozumba teaches at the Department of Philosophy, University of Calabar and is a Professor of Epistemology. His research interests also include African Philosophy and History of Philosophy. He was formerly the chair of philosophy in the University of Calabar. He has written well over sixteen books. He propounded the theory of Integrative Humanism.

Michael Ukah obtained his Ph.D from University of Calabar. He teaches at Michael Okpara University of Agriculture Umudike. He has published in both Local and international journals. He specializes in history of philosophy and socio-political philosophy.

About the Book

In most World Universities where Ancient Western Philosophy is taught the popular genre is to regurgitate the history of Greek Philosophy from maybe, the pre-philosophical period of the poets—Homer and Hesiod and the classical literature that formed the source of early Greek wisdom and from there move on to the dawn of philosophizing blazed by the Milesian Philosophers Thales, Anaximander and Anaximenes through to what is now known as the golden era of Greek philosophy as well as philosophy after Aristotle. This book is therefore written for students of philosophy up to intermediate level as well as for the green-horn researchers from other disciplines. It is comprehensive and simplified.

CHAPTER ONE

THE AGE OF MYTHOLOGY

Historical evolution of any thought proceeds not in isolation but through a process which must have started from a period in time. The achievements of any particular period cannot be a wholly independent occurrence hence it must have some germs of past eras and the congenital and necessary influence. In this wise, one cannot successfully talk about the history of philosophy without first of all falling back to have a look at the period that preceded what we have come to regard as the era of philosophical thought. The kind of thinking which I have the persuasion to call "the age of mythology" could rightly be regarded as such because of the philosophical ingredients which it lacked. But the fact that some questions which fundamentally had some kind of influence on the early philosophers like Thales were asked by these unphilosophical poets gives them a place in the tracing of the origin of Western philosophy.

During the age of myths, the Greek Society was inextricably tied to the apron string of the might of gods. They had a pantheistic view about the universe. They concerned themselves with the origin of the gods (Theogony) and the origin of the universe (cosmogony).

Since in philosophy we deal with a continuum and not with abrupt transitions, it will be pertinent to carry out in-depth analyses of the thought of the poets. With a view to finding out why their views could not pass the test of being philosophical. It must be noted that the fact that the earlier type of thought was propelled by sheer fantasy although it was animated by a desire to find explanations but its mode or criteria which constituted the explanations they gave were very crude and unphilosophical. Before any system of thought can pass for philosophy, it must not only be rational, it must be logical, consistent, coherent, reasonable, systematic and critical. Although the thoughts of these earlier poets may not have lacked all the above named ingredients but there are pointers to show that it was bereft of a substantial number of these key determinants. To this extent, their system could be classified as being mythic and anthropomorphic. Example is the Iliad of Homer. In his Iliad Homer tells about the relationship existing between God and man. He talked about the composition and organization of the Greek kingdom. In Homer's work Zeus was in complete possession of nature with the gods as a kind of Vice regal Suzerainty under Zeus. Zeus was the father of all things. Hesiod was another poet who belonged to this period. He also talked about nature and the gods. He did not, like his forebear, look at the universe with a philosophical telescope and in this manner wandered off the philosophical road to dwell on theology and myths. Although he disagreed with Homer on many issues pertaining to the organization of Greek social structure but the rallying point is that both did not concern themselves with a concrete rational method of inquiry. This crude way of perceiving the universe, denied them the coveted position of being the fathers of Greek philosophy.

Nature of History of Philosophy
The history of philosophy is neither a collection of ideas nor a mere narration of the history of Western philosophy. If it is treated as an enumeration of ideas and opinions, it becomes an idle tale. There is a connection or link between one period and another. It represents a continuous happening marked by action and reaction i.e. thesis and antithesis which at times could extend to a synthesis of the train of thought. To understand better the cause of happenings, you must have to do so within the set i.e. with reference to preceding happenings. There is a logical, though not a necessary sequence from one philosophic theme to another.

The history of philosophy has been geared towards the search for truth by discursive reasoning, not through mythology, superstition, magic or revelation. This also meant the search for the ultimate goal. Many people believe truth to be got at through revelation, while others hold that truth comes through intellectual discussion. The truth is that truth comes through revelation and intellectual discussion. To discard any shows the extent those people lack philosophical insight and in unequivocal terms could be regarded as non compos mentis individuals. In the search for truth, failure might often be attained but this does not imply that we should despair in our search. A philosopher is a searcher after truth, he must open his mind and be receptive of truth through every rational and convinced sources (COPLESTON 1967, 2-12).

Study Approach
This involves the need to see any philosophical reason within the context of its historical setting and connexion. It also includes a certain attempt at sympathy i.e. a psychological insight related to the time of the happening. It demands an attempt to try to know the philosopher not in isolation of the period in which he lived and thought. You do not have to start by viewing a philosopher as having an inferior knowledge and insight. You must strive with no bias in other to embrace without personal prejudices the peculiarities and characteristics inherent in the philosopher. You should place yourself in the position of the philosopher (empathy) and reason with him using the period in which he lived with the prevailing conditions as a measure for your own assessment of him (principle of charity).

Try to know the kind of meaning the philosopher wanted to convey e.g. Plato's "justice" as he used it is different in meaning from its present use. To work yourself into the philosophic system does not mean only understanding the morals and phrases the philosopher uses but there must be an intelligent and consistent insight in the study of the philosophical thoughts of any philosopher (COPLESTON 1967, 8-10).

Phases of Greek Philosophy
Greek philosophy is generally classed into four distinct groups which are as follows:
1. The pre-Socratic era
2. The Golden-Era of Greek philosophy
3. The Hellenistic Period
4. The Roman Period

1. The Pre-Socratic Period
This is the earliest known beginning of philosophy with no surviving words and our source of knowledge is got through fragments in the form of Diels or Doxographies. This period is made up of a group of philosophers called the Ionians.

2. The Golden Era of Greek Philosophy
This period is rightly termed the golden era as it is the greatest era of Greek thought. This period produced the three greatest philosophers of history in the order of their existence – Socrates, Plato and Aristotle. Socrates is the father of this period, with our knowledge of him got through his pupil—Plato. From the last two we have abundance of surviving words.

3. The Hellenistic Period
This is the period after Aristotle and it marked the end of the Polis (city) states. This era witnessed two Schools (1) The stoics and (2) the skeptics and the Epicureans. Both of these periods taught the philosophy of Hedonism or pleasure or the philosophy of Plato.

4. The Roman Period
Here we witnessed a different version of stoicism in Rome, with two prominent names Seneca and Marcus Aurelius. There existed an important development of one of the greatest philosophers of all time Plotinus. The Enneads is a collection of Plotinus' major works. Here also we have St. Augustine of Hippo whose nationality is in dispute. This marks the end of the Roman as well as ancient philosophy.

The Beginning of Nature Philosophy
Greek philosophy was born in the coast of Asia Minor. Ionia and Ephesus being the prominent cities and can be termed Ionian City States. They were the richest and the most highly civilized of all Greek cities distinguished by an attitude of religious detachment and indifferentism. These cities were, originally founded by people from Greek mainland. They sought explanation of things in rationalism rather than in religion and superstition.

In commerce, they lived by sea faring which explains why they were interested in the weather and stars, thus meteorological guideline were needed. They freely made use of astronomical knowledge gained from the Egyptians and further developed on this knowledge. This gave rise to a new type of thinking called philosophy which aided them to escape from ignorance. The Ionians asked a lot of fundamental questions about the world and about the nature of things. Curiosity and the desire to know for its own sake followed by wonder is the true beginning of philosophy. They asked the what, why, who questions about the world.

Their interest in the phenomena of the sun, moon, stars, etc., ended in their inquiry about the genesis of the whole universe. These resulted in asking about the 'why' of things, questions about the ultimate cause of things, which showed that they were already in the domain of wisdom (philosophy). They inquired into the first principle or ultimate cause of things. These represented an attempt to understand all things from the standpoint of human reasoning. The Ionians were the first to bring this inquiry to the point of human knowledge. Thales of Miletus with Anaximander his pupil began what Greek biographers call "the philosophers".

It should however be noted that the Egyptians, Persians and Indians influenced Ionian philosophy but the point of uncertainty lies in the extent of their influence. They were primarily concerned about truth of the universe (cosmos) hence, Greek philosophers are often termed cosmologists (COPLESTON 1967, 14-16)

Three fundamental questions seemed to obsess the minds of these philosophers. The first being the reality of Being. All different things nevertheless have something in common, i.e. that which gives them their existence. In an attempt to answer this question, they sought for the primary or primal element that underlies fundamentally, the structure of everything which is the starting point of science. The second question was directed to man and this is the true beginning of metaphysics.

The third question which they asked was "Do things make any sense? Can we come up with a philosophical system to explain the world?" The Ionian philosophers from Miletus, i.e. Thales, Anaximander and Anaximenes attempted to answer these questions. Greek philosophy it must be noted was born out of the struggle to understand nature and to give rational explanations thereto. Initially, the early Greek philosophers or scientists took for granted the need to look for the material stuff of the universe but later it became clear that there was need to look deeper into the nature of the primordial substance and it was in this regard, that they asked the following questions:

1. What is the original material stuff that makes up the universe?
2. What does it mean to say that something endures through change?
3. What is the relation between the one real stuff and its many appearances?

They asked the above questions because the poets gave contradicting explanations about the nature of the universe and this gave rise to skepticism. But honest curiosity drove the Ionians into a more rational and scientific investigation which enabled them to come up with answers backed up with philosophical reasons. They raised problems in the process of their inquiry and explanations. They are:

1. The problem of appearance and Reality
2. The one and the many
3. Paradoxes about change i.e. change and changeless

Note that before the time of rational, intensive and systematic philosophy, religious myths provided sanctions for socially oriented behaviour but the table was over turned by the advent of the Ionians.

The Ionian philosophers were deeply awed by the possibility of change, which expresses itself in birth and death, day and night, summer and winter, coming into being and passing away, Being and Becoming, etc. It was fundamentally this basic fact of change that drove the Ionians to start philosophizing. They conjectured that despite all this change that take place, that there must be something permanent and they asked the question, why? The answer is that according to them, the process of change must start from something into something. They thought that there must be something primary that underlies this change. Unequivocally one can say that the main obsession of the Ionians was to discover the primary stuff of the universe. Though the Ionians differed in the stuff they chose but all agreed that it must be a material substance. Thales said water, Anaximander chose the unlimited, Anaximenes clung to air while Heraclitus insisted that it must be fire. But at this time, the distinction between matter and spirit had not been drawn or established therefore, they cannot rightly be classified as materialistic furthermore, they went beyond sense to reason in their explanation. Little background will suffice. Greek Philosophy is said to be born in the Ionian city states that dotted the Western coast of Asia Minor. Greeks from the mainland who were fleeing from the Dorian invasion came and settled there and formed these states. These states were situated along the coast of Asia Minor bounded by great waters. This made sea faring and commerce their source of livelihood. This also explains why they were able to develop astronomical, meteorological and geometrical knowledge to help them cope with their natural environment and occupation. This knowledge is said to have been originally gathered from the Egyptians and the Chaldeans. Though, they received this knowledge in their crude form, it was the ingenuity of the Ionians that improved on this inherited knowledge.

Philosophy was a child of curiosity, wonder, and adventure. It resulted from the application of reason in solving human problems or in attempting answers to natural puzzles. This is why Aristotle had to say that inquiries concerning the whys of happenings led to question about the ultimate nature of things and this is the true beginning of philosophy (OWENS 1959, 4).

CHAPTER TWO

THALES OF MILETUS 624-546 BC

He was reportedly the earliest known philosopher to flourish. Accordingly, as the earliest Ionian philosopher he concerned himself with the original stuff of the universe. He reflected about the fact of change and the order that exist in the world. He was credited with many achievements. He predicted the eclipse of 585 BC. He also was of the view that the earth is a flat disc superimposed upon water. To him the primary stuff of all things was water. He was the first to raise the question of the one and the many. He was led to choose water through observation and reason.

He said that since water is the primal substance, that it is the first principle. He says that "the nutrient of all things is moist and that heat itself is generated from the moist and kept alive by it. He said that the seeds of all things have a moist nature and water is the origin of the nature of moist things.

He also observed that nourishment (heat) of every living organism comes from moist things, thus water is the origin of moist. This is based on his observation of natural phenomena. Their questions and answers were new. Before him existed poets who explained things in religious perspective. At this period, there existed the problem of change or motion and this led Thales to look into the question of motion.

Thales is also credited with the sayings that "the Magnet has a Soul that moves Iron" and that "All things are full of gods". Aristotle was the one who wrote about Thales. With the above sayings, he was trying to explain motion i.e. that there is something that is responsible for every movement. Thales explanation of motion is animistic because he believed that things possess souls that move them—this belief could be an influence of the Greek Society in which he lived i.e. world view as was carved out by the poets. There existed the contention that everything changes but the problem is how can something change from what it is to what it is not? This opened the way for the problem of the one and the many.

He said that the soul that moves iron is the source of both motion and life. Thales also looked at the question of stability e.g. man dies and new ones are born daily but human nature cannot change. This means that the species ever remains the same. This leads to the problem of essence and differentiations which in some way later gave rise to the philosophies of existentialism essentialism and naturalism.

The most important conception in Thales philosophy is the belief that things are varying forms of one primary and ultimate element. He also first conceived the notion of unity in difference. In Thales, we witness the transition from myth to science and philosophy. According to Diogenes Laertius, it is said that Thales fell into a well while gazing into the Star for astronomical knowledge. This points to how philosophers neglect immediate problems in preference to some rarefied problems that have little or no relevance to human existence. However, this tale was countered by another which presented Thales as making a fortune through the forecast of bumper harvest of olives. He bought off all that was available and sold later at his own rate and became very rich. This was only to prove a point that Philosophers can be rich if they wanted. Philosophers are rather more interested in meddling with all forms of knowledge (COPLESTON 1967, 22). Other (Philosophers/Historians) like Aristotle, Herodotus, Diogenes Laertius, Owens and Copleston have given very insightful information about Thales.

Thales is therefore, credited with a number of thoughts that are said to have provided impetus for the development of science. (1) The important place of observation in the scientific enterprise. (2) He introduced hypothesis as an important segment of the scientific process. For instance water, water is chosen as the primordial element on which the earth rests. Also, that the seed of all things have a moist nature and that water is the source of plant and animal life. (3) We see Thales' use of the scientific method of testing in validating his claims. He subjected every of his hypothesis to rigorous testing. For example, he recommended that the height of the pyramid can be measured by measuring its shadow when the shadow of a man is equal to the man's height. (4) He is the originator of instrumentalism. He recommended the constellation little bear as the device for knowing the position of the North. (5) Thales was thoroughly pragmatic which is a modern scientific disposition. He successfully divided the Haley's river into two thereby creating two smaller rivers over which it is easier to build bridges, thus enabling the Lydian king's army to cross the Haley's river. (6) Thales displayed the predictive function of science by being the first person to predict an eclipse. He is said to have predicted the eclipse of the sun on 28 May 585BC. (7) We see the imaginative endowment of Thales which led (though falsely to) the view that the magnetic pull of the magnet is an indication of possession of soul. As he says, the magnet has a soul that moves iron. (8) He anticipated the scientific vitalism of the twentieth century by seeing things as constituting of life giving force. He says that "all things are full of gods". This view insinuates even the corpuscular theory of the eighteenth century and the atomism of the atomists and the monadism of Leibniz. These presuppose the existence of life, structure giving forces, elements, substances that animate physical objects. Leibniz calls his monads "souls or metaphysical or spiritual windowless substances which make up all things. (9) We see the materialism of Thales' Postulations. Thales' "water" is material and is seen as the cause of all things. He says that the many are related to each other by one (STUMPF 1971, 4). His scientific procedure began with the observation of natural phenomenon and led back to their ultimate material force (OWENS 1959, 10). This is the real beginning of natural philosophy. This earned Thales the name the Philosopher from Aristotle even though the term Philosopher was first coined by Pythagoras of Samos. (10) The theory of scientific evolutionism could be dimly traced back to Thales transmutation of water into other forms of life. This corresponds to the modern scientific theories of "biogenesis" which considers sea water as the best medium for the formation of organic matter (OWENS 1959, 11) we can conclude by saying that the concept of Western philosophy, science and geography began with Thales. The astronomical, cosmological, cosmogonical, astrological and metaphysical conception of nature is all wrapped up in his natural philosophy.

Part of the reason why we are studying the philosophical thoughts of Thales is to show how early scientific pattern of reasoning began to emerge. Thales is credited with a number of thoughts and activities which conform to the spirit of science. For example, we see

(1) The important place of observation in his philosophical process.

(2) We see the formulation of hypothesis based on observation. For instance, water is chosen as the primordial element on which the earth rests. Also, that the seed of all things have a moist nature and that water is the source of plant and animal life.

(3) We see Thales' use of the scientific method of testing in validating his claims. He subjected every of his hypothesis to rigorous testing. For example, he recommended that the height of pyramid can be measured by measuring its shadow when the shadow of a man is equal to the man's height.

(4) He is the originator of instrumentalism. He recommended the constellation little bear as the device for knowing the position of the North.

(5) Thales was thoroughly pragmatic which is a scientific disposition. He successfully divided the Haley's river into two thereby creating two smaller rivers over which it is easier to build bridges, thus enabling the Lydian King's army to cross the Haley's river.

(6) Thales displayed the predictive function o science by being the first person to predict an eclipse. He is said to have successfully predicted the eclipse of the sun in the 28 May 585 BC.

(7) We see the imaginative endowment of Thales which led (through falsely) to the view that the magnetic pull of the magnet is an indication of possession of soul. As he says "the magnet has a soul that moves iron."

(8) He anticipated the scientific vitalism of the twentieth century by seeing things as constituting of life-giving force. He says that "all things are full of gods".

This view insinuates even the corpuscular theory of the eightieth century. And the atomism of the atomists and the monadism of Leibniz. These presuppose the existence of life, structure giving forces, elements, substances that animate physical objects. Leibniz calls his monads "Souls or metaphysical or spiritual window-less substances which make up all things.

(9) We see the materialism of Thales' postulations. Thales' "water" is material and is seen as the cause of all things. He says that the many are related to each other by one (STUMPF 1971, 4).

His scientific procedure began with the observation of natural phenomenon and led back to their ultimate material force (OWENS 1959, 10). This is the real beginning of natural philosophy. This earned Thales the name the philosopher from Aristotle even though the term "philosopher" was first coined by Pythagoras of Samos.

(10) The theory of scientific evolutionism could be dimly traced back to Thales transmutation of water into other forms of life. This corresponds to the modern scientific theories of "biogenesis" which considers sea water the best medium for the formation of organic matter (OWENS 1959, 11).

We can conclude by saying that the concept of western philosophy, science and geography began with Thales – the astronomical, cosmogonical, cosmological, astrological and metaphysical conception of nature are all wrapped up in his natural philosophy.

CHAPTER THREE

ANAXIMANDER OF MILETUS 610-546 BC

Anaximander is known as the younger contemporary and pupil of Thales (STUMPF 1971, 6). Owens describes him as the countryman, pupil, associate and successor of Thales. He is placed in the generation following that of Thales. He continued with the natural investigation inaugurated by Thales. What we know of him is from Theophrastus. He busied himself with practical scientific pursuits. The Ionians being seafarers and sailors benefited from the scientific achievements of Anaximander. He constructed the first known map for their use. Like Thales, Anaximander devoted his time to search for the ultimate stuff of the universe. In the process of his investigation, he came to the conclusion that the particular stuff of Thales cannot be the original substance because of some inherent inconsistencies. He wondered how a particular thing could give rise to the multifarious things that evidently exist in the universe.

To him, since water is an aspect of the opposites, it cannot give rise to other opposites. This is so because what is an opposite of something cannot be that thing neither can it produce or be the origin of that thing. Water being an opposite of say Solid substance cannot be the same or the source of their origination. In the first place, the conflicts and encroachments are themselves in need of explanation. It must be remembered that though Anaximander agreed with Thales that there is one real, basic stuff, that is in process, he differed with Thales both about what this stuff is and about the nature of the process by which it becomes many. What Anaximander's contention is, is that nothing particular can give rise to the sundry things in the universe. He was of the view that anything that has the capacity for producing all other things must also have the capacity for accommodating those other things. He says that since water is too specific, that it cannot possibly be the reservoir of all the multitudinous things we have in the world.

He, therefore, conceived of Thales argument as deficient in terms of not being consistent. To him, there is a logical contradiction in Thales mode of operation or framework. It was because of this reason that Anaximander proceeded to modify his own framework to meet the logical difficulty which enveloped Thales' own.

Anaximander, it should be noted was not quarrelling with Thales "water" only but was of the view that any other determinate stuff will have the same difficulty e.g. air, earth and fire. He, therefore, argued that the one stuff must be without particular limiting characteristics, it was this that led him to hold that the one stuff must be the infinite, the unlimited or the boundless. He however adhered or followed the basic assumptions of Thales

1. That there must be one ultimate stuff
2. That there must be a process by which the one becomes the many things in the world
3. That this process must be a necessary one

Anaximander in his own explanation was more specific in that he looked more perspicuous in talking about the world process. He says that the one real stuff i.e. the boundless gives rise to the numerous things that exist in this world and that all this particulars are bound to return to the boundless. He conceived of the boundless as a reservoir.

Anaximander examined the pairs of opposites like hot and cold, wet and dry, day and night, etc., and saw them as basic realities of nature. He went further to explain why these opposites are perpetual. At this point he brought in the law of reparation for injustice. This exchange happens with a regularity that seemed to Anaximander to imply some sort of compulsion. Anaximander without gainsaying any fact witnessed disorderliness staring him at the face but he was confused about the underlying orderliness which indubitably exists. He tried to explain this with the introduction of the boundless and reparation for injustice. To him, particulars come and disappear into the boundless because of the injustice they commit against each other. So things come and pass out of existence in an orderly manner. His boundless is ageless and without limits, it encompasses all the worlds.

To Anaximander the original source of all these changes is the unlimited, though you can't identify it with any of these changes it is stable, from it issues all the multiplicity of things that we see in the cosmos. The unlimited is eternal, ageless, deathless and indestructible, it encompasses and steers all things, it is inexhaustible in a quantitative sense and it is an inexhaustible reservoir for cosmic development to mark the generation of all things. The opposites are contained in the unlimited. Eternal motion is an attribute of the unlimited (the unmoved mover) none of these elements of change is predominant and none can be used to qualify the unlimited.

It is with Anaximander that the course of observable change began in real earnest. The phenomenal observation of one thing changing into another was continued by him. Also, he continued with the Milesian tradition of finding the primitive vital stuff as the origin of the universe. He highlighted the problem of particulars and universals. In the process of change, there can be perceptive order which emanates from the eternal motion of the unlimited. The doctrine of Anaximander shows advancement in thought from where Thales stopped. He proceeded from one determinate element to an indeterminate element as the first principle.

Anaximander's philosophical teachings can be summarized thus: (1) that water is too specific to be the origin of all things. (2) Water is limited and cannot account for the source of limitless things in nature. (3) Water being specific and limited cannot generate its opposite. (4) That water represents only the liquid form of substance and cannot account for the gaseous and the solid state of existence. (5) That water cannot account for the principle of eternal justice which is responsible for the harmony among opposites. Theophrastus records one of his surviving fragments which reads thus: "The first principle of existing things is the unlimited… but into those from which the existing things have their coming to be, do they also pass away according to necessity, for they give justice and make amends to one another for their injustice according to the ordering of time" (OZUMBA 1996, 53-54) (OWENS 1959, 13). From the above quotation we see the principles of harmony, justice, necessity, unlimited and time.

Anaximander's Contributions to the Development of Science

We can say that Anaximander enunciated serious thinking in the procedure of science. We see his logicality, coherence, superior reasoning, consistency and comprehensiveness of thought. We can, therefore, summarize his contributions to the development of science as follows: (1) Anaximander is said to be the father of organic evolution. He postulated that all life originated from water and man originated from fish. That man is incapable of surviving on dry ground due to long nurturing (gestation) period. (2) He is said to have drawn the first map. (3) He is the father of astronomy. He is noted to have talked about the formation of the various universes and the stars. (4) His theory of reparation and the eternal motion can be said to have influenced the theories of motion of Aristotle and even later scientists.

He is famed for his theory of conservation of energy for nothing is actually formed or destroyed. All things return to the inexhaustible reservoir of all things from which they originated in the first place. Anaximander's philosophical thoughts have been criticized for being more abstract than that of Thales. What he means by the indeterminate boundless is not known. Could that be the equivalent of the Christian God or a type of Deus ex machine for explaining away the nature of things? Though he proposes a materialistic conception of the universe; his terms are hardly materialistic. The real question was that of finding the specific origin of all things. This he overlooked and concerned himself with the indeterminate that is neither here nor there. He is also criticized for not fully explaining his evolutionary process. It was Plutarch who embellished his view that men came from fish to mean that the original man developed fully in the womb of the fish and was vomited after being fully grown and then allowed to fend for him. In summary, evolutionary theory is an unsubstantiated hypothesis.

His Philosophical Teachings
Anaximander objected to Thales primordial substance "water" on the following grounds:
(1)   That water was too specific to be the origin of all things.
(2)   Water is limited and cannot account for the source of limitless things in nature.
(3)   Water being specific and limited cannot generate its opposite.
(4)   That water represents only the liquid form of substance and cannot account for the gaseous and the solid state of existence.
(5)   That water cannot account for the principle of eternal justice which is responsible for the harmony among opposites.

Theophrastus records one of his surviving fragments which reads thus "The first principle of existing things is the unlimited – but into those from which the existing things have their coming to be, do they also pass away according to necessity, for they give justice and make amends to one another for their injustice according to the ordering of time" (OWENS 1959, 13). From the above quotation, we see the principles of harmony, justice, necessity, unlimited and time. These are very central in Anaximander's philosophical teachings.

Deviating from Thales' "water" he propounded that the elementary substance out of which all things come, is what he calls the unlimited or the indeterminate boundless or the Apeiron. His argument is that, whereas actual things are specific, their origin cannot be specific but indeterminate. The innumerable finite can only come from the infinite boundless. He talks about the necessity for a cosmic reservoir which not only can be the source of all things, but should contain all things. All things emanate from this boundless reservoir and to it they return.

Anaximander's postulations are said to be superior to those of Thales. He is said to have provided a better hypothesis for explaining the fact of one and the many, unity in diversity, change and changeless. He talks of the concept of eternal fire, the whirling and separating off of specific objects from the indeterminate which gives rise to different things while the eternal fire (the principles of justice) remains the same, it gives use to the different existent things. He enunciated the concept of original motion which give rise to the separating off. He talks about the conflicts of opposites and the reconciliation and harmonization of these conflicts. The eternal action gives rise to cosmic process. We have such opposites as right and day, life and death, hot and cold etc. For him, from the eternal motion came the heavens (through a separating off process) then, we have warm and cold, then we have moist (water) then air and from air other elements came to be. It is in this light that Anaximander's teachings are said to transcend those of Thales. Because, it accounts for the origin of water itself and goes beyond it.

      His inexhaustible reservoir accounts for dynamics of qualitative and quantitative changes in existent things – this, Thales water cannot fully explain. He talked about the concept of reparation. All things make reparation for their injustice according to the ordering of time. One important lesson we learn is the fact that time heals all wounds and harmonies all conflicts even in human relations.

CHAPTER FOUR

ANAXIMENES OF MILETUS 528 – 525 B.C

Anaximenes was the third philosopher of the Milesian School. He was an associate, pupil and a necessary successor of Anaximander. Anaximenes posited that all the diversity of things we see in the world are reducible to one stuff and that is "air" thereby returning to Thales conception that the ultimate stuff must be a particular thing. Because of this fact of returning to the perception of Thales, many people have tended to regard his doctrines as a decided retrogression from the stage reached by Anaximander. He was therefore regarded as going backwards instead of improving on the advancement made by Anaximander. But Anaximenes' reasons could be regarded as being plausible because the point at issue is the discovery and enunciation of a particular thing which is the original stuff of the universe. But Anaximander in defiance of this all important objective left the inquiry into a particular thing to dwell on a boundless substance as his first principle thereby subverting the set purpose of the Milesian inquiry. It must be noted that Anaximander defined his first stuff as the boundless, the unlimited, and the indeterminate. He failed to tell us exactly what his boundless stood for. And since his boundless had no limited characteristics, it cannot be regarded as a particular thing. To Anaximenes, to be a thing is to have a particular characteristic and since Anaximander's boundless is not a thing and hence without characteristics, it cannot be the one stuff of the universe—since it is not classifiable. With the basic hypothesis or propositions of Anaximander, one can find that the proposition of Anaximander that all things come from one material stuff which is boundless is in conflict. This is so because the boundless which is not a thing cannot be a particular stuff that makes up the world. The boundless hence is not a particular things and the only stuff must be a particular thing. The boundless posited by Anaximander does not solve the problem but only conceals the existence of a problem or exacerbates the problem.

Refutation
Anaximenes purports to suggest that it is either that the boundless of Anaximander is a grab-bag collection of the particular stuffs in which case it is not a thing or a particular stuff but a concatenation of things or particular stuffs which discards monism and places it at a disadvantage; or, it is an indefinite something which being nothing in particular, is nothing at all.

Viewing Anaximenes philosophy one could say that it was improper for people to view it as a "draw back" sort of thing but as a tremendous advancement or enhancement of Thales philosophy which is head and shoulder above that of Anaximander. The judgment of which view is better than the other can only be done from different vantage positions depending on our points of interest and argumentation.

Anaximenes is quoted to have said that "Just as our Soul being air keeps us together, so do breathe and air encompass the whole world. As air controls humanity so does it control the ordered universe". He explains this by the process of condensation and rarefaction.

Condensation and Rarefaction
He agrees with his master that the primal substance is one and unlimited, but differs by saying that it is not indeterminate rather it is determinate Air. Through the process of condensation and rarefaction, air becomes the different things in the universe. When air is rarefied i.e. made lighter you get fire. But when condensed you get wind, cloud, water, earth, stone, etc. All these take place through an eternal motion of air. Motion is intrinsic to the primal substance and this is responsible for the cosmic development which it engenders. Jones puts it this way "when air is dilated into a rarer form, it becomes fire; while on the other hand, air that is condensed forms wind. If this process goes further, it gives water, still further

earth, and the greatest condensation of all is found in stones (JONES 1970, 13).

To Anaximenes the earth is flat like a table and is borne by air. As the vast expanse of Thales' water surrounds the land, so do Anaximenes' unlimited expanse of air surrounds both water and the world. Air is invisible but becomes visible through "the cold, the hot, the wet and the moving". Note that Anaximenes' air though boundless is different from the boundless of Anaximander because his own is specific, tangible and one.

Ionian Contributions to Philosophy
The Ionian philosophers made immense and appreciable contributions to the growth of Western philosophy because they started what we can call systematic philosophy. They initiated a reflective and rational investigation into the ultimate composition of nature and in this way unraveled many things which constituted philosophical problems which they in their own way tried to find answers to. Unlike the poets, they were able to differentiate between religious ideas and concrete philosophizing. They pursued their investigations with a free, unprejudiced and scientific spirit. They avoided the half scientific and half philosophic reflections of the poets and embraced all the ingredients that make up philosophy like being logical, coherent, systematic, reflective, consistent and thorough within the context of the period they philosophized. They raised problems which are important in philosophical circles and these are:
1. The explanation of the world process
2. The problem of the one and the many
3. The problem of change
4. The problem of unity in diversity
5. The problem of particulars and universals

They also looked at the question of limited and unlimited. Anaximenes laid the basis for a quantitative description of the world.

In general the main importance of the Ionians lies not only in the answers they gave but in the questions they asked as to the ultimate nature of things. The answers they gave were verifiable. A controversy arose over the type of answers they gave in material objects which led some people to describe them as materialists. But at this time, there existed no distinction between matter and spirit which proves it wrong to call them dogmatically, materialists. In a sense they were materialists by trying to explain everything in material objects. It should also be noted that the Ionians applied the method of reductionism in seeking solutions to the problems they raised. They most importantly opened the way for subsequent philosophers on how philosophical issues ought to be followed. They asked the why, the how and what questions about the universe. All in all, they made remarkable and inaugurative in-road into the spheres of knowledge like philosophy, Geometry, mathematics, theory of evaluation, Engineering, Geography, Science, Metaphysics and Epistemology. They opened the way into all spheres of knowledge for all future scientists and philosophers.

CHAPTER FIVE

XENOPHANES OF COLOPHON 570-478 B.C

Colophon is an inland city of Ionia and is the birth place of Xenophanes. Few of his writings (which appear as fragments) remain. He is rhapsodist (a writer of epic poems). He is said to have lived reciting his own poems instead of the Homeric epics recited by the traditional rhapsodists (Owens 23). He took exception to the anthropomorphic presentation of the gods in Homeric epics. He saw it as shameful where the actions of the gods are depicted in sordid ways. He was very offended that athletes received greater reward for their performance while he received only a pittance for his more valuable craft of enlightening the soul.

His Philosophical Teachings
For Xenophanes the primary matter is Earth. As he says, "All things that come into being and grow are earth and water". He says that we all are born of earth and water.

His Theological Views
He says that there is a god that is the greatest among all gods and men. Is this god the Almighty God or is it the god Zeus which is regarded as the greatest god in Greek pantheon of gods? He says that this god "sees as a whole, thinks as a whole and hears as a whole". He says that this god "without toil sets everything in motion by the thought of his mind". This god does not move and it is not fitting for him to change his position from time to time (OWENS 1959, 24).

His Epistemological Views
Xenophanes states that "no man has seen the truth nor will there ever be any who knows about the gods and all things that I mention". Even when we say the truth, we never can understand it as the whole truth because we know in part as men. He is the precursor of modern day skepticism and anticipated the theological position of monotheism and its pervasions in polytheism.

CHAPTER SIX

HERACLITUS OF EPHESUS 540 – 480 B.C

He was an Ionian from the city of Ephesus. The background of his thought will be found in Ephesus. He held all philosophical ideas before him in absolute contempt. Knowledge of him is got through fragments. He is remembered for his saying that "change is the law of all being".

Heraclitus tried to answer the question which Thales raised and that is "what is the stuff out of which the world is made"? According to Heraclitus the stuff is fire. To him "the world is now and ever shall be an everlasting fire". Heraclitus was obviously influenced by the Milesian thinkers. Another Question Heraclitus faced was "how can the one change into the many?" Another Question is "how can something give rise to another thing that has different characteristics?" As long as the world is one it would seem to be impossible for it also to be many things. And if it is many how can it be one? Anaximenes had tried to clear up this puzzle. Anaximenes theory merely gives the conditions under which something "air" becomes something else (fire, earth, water) but he does not say what it means to say that air becomes water. Heraclitus says that unless air remains air throughout the process of rarefaction and condensation, it cannot be said to be the one stuff, instead it will be regarded as the many. To Heraclitus the world is one only in the sense of being an ordered cosmos. Taking cognizance of deficiencies that bedeviled the earlier philosophies, Heraclitus thought over the past one stuff of preceding philosophers and came up with the view that it is only fire that can take charge of the problem of the one and the many. It is only fire that while remaining the same, gives the apparition of change. Heraclitus was of the view that one cannot step into the same river twice and that change was a fact of life. This statement was later improved by his disciple Cratylus that "you could not step into the same river even once". All things are in a state of perpetual flux and change. How then can we here in the universe be able to find reality that is eternal, restful, unchanging, and stable. "Perpetual conflict and war is the father of all things". The clash of opposites is the very condition of life. Heraclitus' puzzle of flux was explained in the example he gave. He said that water is continuously flowing; similarly the desk and chairs are in a state of flux, their appearance of permanence results from the fact that their rate of change is constant. Example, it is just like water was running into and out of swimming pool at a constant rate, thereby keeping the water level the same.

Heraclitus continues by saying that evil and good, hot and cold, wet and dry, etc., are opposites and each necessarily compliments the other; and the endless strife (war) between these opposites is the sum of existence. The only harmony possible is the harmony of conflict and contrast produced by opposite tensions. Every pair of opposites is indivisible and equally natural and necessary, one without the other is impossible. Heraclitus means that without the balance of opposing forces society will disappear in civil war.

Heraclitus is opposed to Pythagoras and others who were looking for the eternal and unchanging substance of the universe. Note that the world of perpetual change and conflict pictured by Heraclitus is not a mere chaos. He says that the world is governed by an immanent principle of order and measure and his name for this principle is "logos".

What is Logos?
Logos is the universal proportion of the mixture, the law or principle of the measure and just order which affects the harmony of opposing things. Logos is law because it is a living all ruling intelligence which seems to be identified with the ever living fire; which is the stuff of the universe, as Heraclitus says, "the thunder bolt steers all things". The fire of Heraclitus is ever living but not immortal, transformable into all things and all things into it.

Logos is the universal principle which is the cause of order in the universe. Also, it is the cause of rationality and harmony.

Logos is Heraclitus greatest contribution to the inheritance of thought.

Heraclitus had extraordinary intuition of the nature of the world in which we live, a world in which all things are subject to the law of perpetual change, in which things come into existence and pass away and in which the only possible harmony is a delicate and precarious tension of opposing forces but all the same a world which is no mere chaos but one governed by a living law within change there is order due to the ever living Logos. Everything is fire in that everything is involved in an eternal process of change and exchange.

His Philosophical Teachings

Heraclitus was concerned with explaining why we have unit in diversity. Why do things change while some of their aspects remain the same. The acorn grows into the oak tree, the boy grows into a man, what is living eventually dies and decays. For him his principle of change cannot be explained by Thales' "water" nor Anaximenes' "Air". He therefore posited fire as the primal element. Why fire? He says that fire is simultaneously a deficiency and a surplus. Fire is a process of transformation whereby what is fed into it in transformed into something else.

He is credited with the following saying, "that the world is an ever living fire" characterized by "measures of it kindly and measures going out". "All things are an exchange for fire and fire for all things" (STUMPF 1977, 13-14).

This led to his ideas about change or flux. He says that all things are in a state of flux. Things are ever changing, nothing ever remains the same. He is credited with the saying that "we cannot step into the same river twice because fresh waters are ever coming upon us". This means that things are steadily undergoing changes, nothing ever remains the same. Nothing is eternal substantive and enduring except the law of change itself and "the ever living fire" Fire is responsible for the change from water to Air and from air to earth.

We talked about Reason (Logos) as the universal law. All things are ordered by the universal law. This eternal law guides all things, permeates all things and ensures cosmic orderliness. He sees everything animate and inanimate as consisting of spark of the divine reason. The divine spark or fire is part of all things. This is a type of pantheism.

He is known for his theory about the conflict of opposites. He sees strife as the very essence of change itself. Strife is not evil as most men think. The conflict of opposites is not a calamity but the permanent condition of all things. He is credited with the saying that "war is common and justice is strife and that all things happen by strife and necessity". This means that for Heraclitus change, war, conflict, strife, tension are endemic in the nature of all things. The turning of the lyre entails the conflict of opposites. This means that harmony comes through conflict. After war then comes peace and after conflict comes rest. Nothing is evil in itself-Nature is an unending symphony of conflict and resolution (STUMPF 1977, 15).

In conclusion, we can see that Heraclitus has been able to show us the way out of the problem of change and changeless, unity in diversity, one and the many. The principle of change and conflict is the principle of all things, change and conflict are eternal, perpetual. Fire (eternal logos) through the process of a measure kindling and a measure going out ensures a just cosmic order and also we saw the concept of change and the implication of instability and uncertainty in knowing. Since things are in a state o perpetual flux, to have knowledge of them is impossible. Heraclitus' position is contrasted with the position of Parmenides who himself was an apostle of permanence, being and changelessness.

CHAPTER SEVEN

PARMENIDES OF ELEA 515-456 BC

With him we are in an entirely different atmosphere and epoch. Geographically Elea is in South Italy. He was a younger contemporary of Heraclitus. About him we have two extant fragments (1) The way of truth and (2) The way of opinion. According to Armstrong, the most striking thing about Parmenides is that "he is the first Greek philosopher who reasons". This is because earlier thinkers made no attempt to base their picture of the universe upon logical reasoning or to defend it by rational argument. The logic of Parmenides is the starting point of Platonic dialectic, Aristotelian syllogism and the whole foundation of Western reasoning.

Parmenides started on a monist premise that reality is fundamentally one, that reality is a solid, homogenous sphere. He said that the very notion of change is self-contradictory. All appearances of change and motion are to him illusory.

Basic Propositions

He said that whatever exists could not have come from nothing and on this strength must have come from what exists. But if the existent can come only from the existent, then there is no beginning to what exists and deductively, reality is then eternal and indestructible.

He, therefore, propagated the view that "that which is, is and it is impossible for it not to be". This is the way of truth. Change is absolutely unthinkable and thought cannot follow the way of not-Being. Parmenides rejects the stand of earlier philosophers such as the coming into being and the passing away of things.

For him the word "is", has one sense, and it is the most absolute. "Is" is the whole of actually existing reality and nothing else. This simply means that there is no change. It should be noted at this juncture that Parmenides' propositions were hypothetical in the sense that it was propounded on the condition that it is the One that is in question. This means that if the one is the reality, then to say the many again will be self contradictory. He contends that (1) Being is one, non-Being cannot be. Being is one, changeless and motionless and this is the way of truth.

A is A, "Is is Is and is does not admit of its negation". To accept Parmenides stance is to deny plurality and concomitantly affirming the reality of unity i.e. the one. He says that if there is more than one thing, the one thing will be the other which is a contradiction i.e. if one thing can be another thing then there is a contradiction being therefore is not subject to change. To him what we can perceive is what is and it is impossible to perceive what is not nor think of it. It is only what can be thought that can be.

Parmenides Arguments against Plurality

1. To say that something changes, something must arise out of Being or non Being
2. If it arises out of non-Being, it is contradictory for something cannot arise out of nothing
3. If it arises out of Being, it is not the case because Being is one. Being is uncreated; it exists for all time and without end. Being is continuous and absolute.

Note that Parmenides system is anchored on the thesis of monism which started with Thales and in logical pursuit of the ideals of his predecessors he was led to the conclusions which he arrived at. If monism is true, i.e. the one ultimate stuff of water, air, fire, etc., then the corollary is the truth of conservation of stuff i.e. the eternal, indestructible nature of that stuff. It was these assumptions that led Parmenides to doggedly refuse to distinguish between the qualities of a thing and the thing per se. These consequently led him to uphold the unreality of change. Parmenides rebuttal of the evident fact of change came in his argument that for motion to be possible, that there must be empty space which he religiously denied.

Why Parmenides insists that Being is indivisible is because for being to be divided it has to be divided by something other than itself. But Being cannot be divided by something other than itself' for besides Being there is nothing. Nor can anything be added to it, since anything that was added to Being would itself be Being. Similarly, it is immovable and continuous, for all movements and change forms of becoming are excluded (COPLESTON 1967, 50).

Criticisms

Parmenides chose radically and blindly to reason against sense experience. He was the first to state that reality is attainable by reason only but this is not absolutely true. Although he was the person who presented the problem of the one and the many in its sharpest and clearest terms, he destroyed the old natural philosophy in which a living and changeable one evolve naturally into many beings of the world that we know. It is, therefore, evident that Parmenides philosophy is fraught with some internal problems and the most obvious is the fact that it is not sufficient to reject sense experience as illusion unless one can at least show the possibility of explaining, consistently with one's general position how the illusion occurs and this much needed explanation is lacking in the system of Parmenides. Parmenides' position on illusion suggests the existence of mind, and if mind exists, then it implies that change exist since the mind always goes from one thought to another. Parmenides could therefore be regarded as saying what he said without knowing the implications. His brand of thinking has made people to term him the father of idealism but this is disputable.

The Beginning of the Mathematical Conception of the Universe: Pythagoras of Samos 580 – 570 BC

Pythagoras was born in Samos between 580 and 570BC. His birth and background are shrouded in some mystery. Some fables assign him the place of a saint, a worker of miracles and a teacher of more than human wisdom. His life has been somewhat exaggerated. The fact however remains that the fables indicate that he was an extraordinarily endowed personality. He was the founder of a sect and his followers are called the Pythagoreans. His people looked upon his greatness and popularity as an influence coming from his Western education. However, others see him as having borrowed his philosophy from the East The fact of the proximity of Samos to Egypt reinforces the belief that he not only travelled extensively in Egypt but also studied under the feet of the Egyptian mystery Masters. It was the vogue for people to travel to Egypt for deeper knowledge. Pythagoras saw Philosophers as those who despised avarice and vanity and pursued profound wisdom and the study of nature. He is said to have organized his disciples into a kind of cult where they were enjoined not to eat meat, beans and things that could defile them. Members underwent series of initiations geared at purifying them. Pythagoras was chiefly occupied with the determination of extension and gravity and the measuring of the ratios of musical notes. The Pythagoreans were interested in the study of immaterial and eternal things. Their method is purely deductive and abstractive.

Samos was an Island on the Ionian coast. Pythagoras himself was an Ionian whose life is still shrouded in obscurity. He was said to have visited Egypt, India and many other places where he was fascinated by mathematics. Our source of Pythagoras is from Aristotle who said in his metaphysics that the Pythagoreans devoted themselves to the study of mathematics and were the first to advance it and were also brought up in mathematical schools. They believed that the principles of mathematics were the principles of all things. They were struck by the importance of numbers in the world. For them all things are numbers and it is this that forms the theme of the Pythagorean philosophy. They discovered that musical intervals between notes on the lyre may be expressed numerically. They said that pitch depends on number.

Just as musical harmony is dependent on numbers, they thought that the harmony of the universe also depends on numbers. The Milesian cosmology spoke of the conflict of opposites in the universe. Pythagoras had a solution which brought in the concept of numbers. For them therefore, number is the first principle, the first thing in the universe. Pythagoras combined Anaximander's unlimited with the notion of the limited which gives form to the unlimited. Pythagoras transferred to the world at large what they conceived as musical harmony now conceived as cosmic harmony.

Things are numbers

1. What did they mean by numbers?
2. What did they mean by the statement "All things are numbers?"

Aristotle quoted them as saying that the elements of numbers are the even and the odd. The even is unlimited, the odd is limited. The number 1 (one) proceeds from both the even and the odd. Number here is conceived in a spatial sense.

1   is a point
2   is a line
3   is a surface
4   is a solid

This only happens if points are juxtaposed. To say that all things are numbers means that all bodies consists of points or units in space which when taken together constitute a number, Pythagoreans had a figure called TETRAKTYS, a figure regarded by them as sacred.

This indicates that ten is the sum of one, two, three and four in other words the sum of the first four integers. They represent numbers using pebbles which shows why we had the square and oblong numbers. If you start with one and add odd numbers successively you get square numbers e.g. 1, 3, 5 etc.

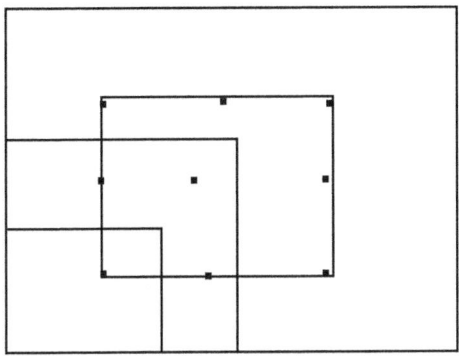

And if you start with two and add even numbers successively, you get oblong numbers.

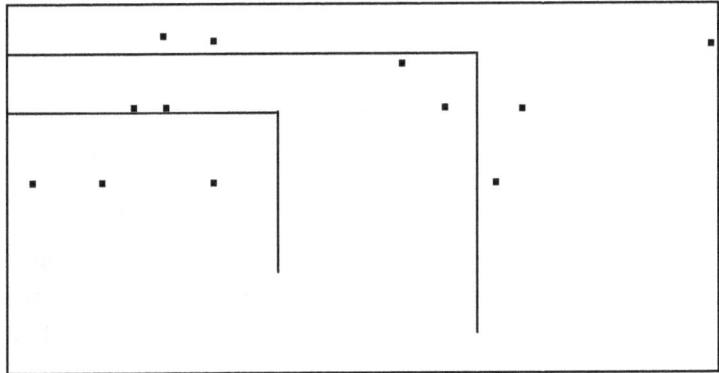

The use of figured numbers or connection of numbers with geometry clearly illustrates how the Pythagoreans regarded things as numbers and not merely numerals. With this connection of numbers with geometry Pythagoras sets a pace of making the first in road into the study of geometry.

By the juxtaposition of several points, a line is generated not just in the scientific imagination but in the external world. And proceeding from this by juxtaposition of several lines, a surface is generated. A body (solid) is generated by the combination of several surfaces. Points, lines and surfaces are therefore the real units which compose all bodies in nature and in this sense all bodies must be regarded as numbers. If objects are regarded as sums of quantitative points and if numbers are regarded geometrically as sums of points, therefore it becomes easy to identify objects with numbers.

The Pythagoreans say that the unlimited cosmos is surrounded by the unlimited boundless Air which it inhales. The objects of the limited cosmos are just not pure limitations there is also a mixture of the unlimited.

Numbers considered as even and odd are products of the unlimited and limited. They held that the earth was spherical and is the centre of the universe and that the earth and the other planets revolve with the sun round the central fire or hearth of the universe. This hearth was identified with the number 1.

They were disturbed as well by the problems posed by change. In trying to solve this, they were very eclectic (accommodating) but instead of naming one object as a primal substance, they chose to call it numbers. They did not materialize their concept (numbers) but rather broke away from the Milesian cosmologists i.e. their materialist conception of the one.

They considerably influenced Plato in his theory of knowledge. They influenced Greek philosophers by propounding a quantitative explanation of the universe. With them began the mathematical and quantitative conception of the universe. In the field of medicine with the help of his mysticism and extra ordinary insight, he was able to use his idea of the mean in health attunement. He conceived of health as an attunement and harmony of opposites. "The body he said is in health when it is neither too hot nor too cold but is in a mean between having a chill and having a fever". It was during this time, that the traditional notion of moderation received a precise and formal treatment.

CHAPTER EIGHT

THE BEGINNING OF DIALECTICS

Zeno of Elea 465 – 455 B.C

Zeno was a pupil of Parmenides. Here we shall concern ourselves with Zeno's analyses of the theories of his master and his paradoxes. Zeno was the author of many paradoxes intended to show the impossibility of change, motion i.e. change of place. He says that the concept of change is self contradictory. To appreciate the effort of Zeno, and to understand him, we have to look at the criticisms of the one propounded by anti-parmenideans. His wise tricks and arguments were not merely witty toys but were calculated to improve the position of his master Parmenides. Since plurality and motion seem to be evident in sense experience, the position of Parmenides really induced ridicule and contempt.

    Zeno, an adherent of Parmenides, tried to improve the theory and position of Parmenides or at least, to show that it is by no means ridiculous. He had to do this by showing that it is the plurality of Pythagoras that is involved in insoluble difficulties. Zeno wanted to show that motion and change which his master regarded as illusory, are impossible even on the pluralist hypothesis. From Proclus a Neo-Platonist we learn that Zeno composed forty proofs to demonstrate (A) that Being is one and (B) that change and motion are impossible. By so doing Zeno showed that the position of the advocates of change like Heraclitus and Pythagoras is even more ridiculous and unacceptable when compared with that of Parmenides. Zeno in some measure used his paradoxes to strengthen the position of Parmenides.

    Aristotle in his version of one of the arguments put forward by Zeno interpreted Zeno as saying that before any distance can be traversed or crossed, that half of that distance must be traversed first. Also these half distances are infinite because any given half in turn consists of its own half. And it is impossible to traverse distances that are infinite in number. For example, if one has to leave his chair to walk to the door he will have to traverse infinite distances and this although we tend to think that we are capable of accomplishing constitutes self delusion as we can never even cover any distance since the distance is infinite.

Proofs against the Many (Pluralism of Pythagoras)

ARGUMENT 1: Supposes that reality is made up of units. Suppose that units are either with or without magnitude. If units are with magnitude, then a line as made up of units possessed of magnitude will be infinitely divisible. Since no matter how you divide, the units will still have magnitude and so will be divisible, but in this case, the line will be made up of an infinite number of units each of which is possessed of magnitude. The line then must be infinitely great since it is composed of infinite number of units. Following this argument therefore it follows that everything in the world must be infinitely great. Therefore the world itself must be infinitely great. Suppose that units are without magnitude, then the whole universe will also be without magnitude since however many units you will add together, if non of them has any magnitude then the collection of them will also be without magnitude.

But if the universe is without any magnitude, it must be infinitely small. Indeed, everything in the universe must be infinitely small. The conclusion that seems to follow from the following, that is, for the proponents of plurality or the many are faced with dilemma i.e. that is either that everything in the universe is infinitely great or that everything in the universe is infinitely small— Namely that the universe and everything in it is infinitely divisible.

The conclusion which Zeno wants to draw is that the supposition from which the dilemma flows is an absurd supposition namely that the universe and everything in it are composed of units [suppose that reality is made up of units, suppose again that units are without magnitude it therefore means that the universe is without magnitude.

ARGUMENT 2: If there is a many, then we ought to be able to say how many they are, at least they should be numerable, if they are not numerable how can they exist? On the other hand, if they cannot possibly be numerable but must be infinite—why? Between any two assigned units there will always be other units just as a line is infinitely divisible. But it is absurd to say that the many are finite in number and infinite in number at the same time.

Against Motion

ARGUMENT 3: The most celebrated arguments of Zeno are those against motion. Again his attempt is to show that motion which Parmenides denied is impossible on the thesis of pluralism. Argument 3A— Suppose you want to cross a stadium or a race course, in order to do so you have to traverse an infinite number of points. Moreover, you have to travel the distance in a finite time. But how can you traverse an infinite number of points and so an infinite distance in a finite time. You cannot cross the stadium; by extension no object can traverse any distance whatsoever and because of this all motion is consequently impossible.

Argument 3B— Paradox of the Achilles and the Tortoise: Suppose that Achilles and the Tortoise are going to have a race. Because Achilles is a good athlete (sportsman), he gives the Tortoise a start. By the time Achilles reaches the point where Tortoise is, the Tortoise has moved another point further. The slower moves as fast as the faster, therefore it is impossible for Achilles ever to overtake the Tortoise as space is infinitely divisible and cannot be traversed.

These arguments are not mere sophistries (i.e. argument with intent to deceive) but are ingenious tricks put forward to discredit the proponents of the many and motion.

ARGUMENT 4: Another argument is that against the Pythagorean doctrine of space. He says that if things must be in space to exist as Pythagoras held, that it follows that for the existence of space to be possible, that there must be a space in which that space exists, and that space will in turn need another space and this continues indefinitely. To Zeno this kind of thing amounts to absurdity and incongruity (not in agreement with what we know).

ARGUMENT 5: Another argument against motion is that of the Arrow. According to Pythagoras, things occupy space. And if an arrow has to occupy a position in space, it means that it is at rest because to be at rest is to occupy a position in space. But we know that a flying arrow always occupies a position in space and this leads us to conclude that a flying arrow is both at rest and in motion and this is an absurd and unacceptable conclusion.

Zeno's Position
Zeno was of the view that reality is a complete kind of thing without the possibility of empty spaces. He conceived reality as a continuum and a plenum without pockets and this led him to advocate the impossibility of motion and the many. His dialectics and his reductio-ad-absurdum method were not essentially meant to establish the monism of his master which was exposed to insuperable objections but was poised to show that the pluralist's hypothesis on which the theory of the many and motion are entrenched lead to palpable absurdities.

CHAPTER NINE

AN OVERVIEW OF ANCIENT PHILOSOPHY

1. **The Eleatics**

The Eleatics denied the reality of multiplicity and motion. There is only one principle according to them and that is Being which they conceived of as motionless and unchanging. They did not deny that we sense multiplicity and change but tenaciously held that what we sense is illusion i.e. mere appearance. To them true Being can be found not by sense experience but by thought and thought shows that there can be no plurality, change nor motion. They, like their predecessors attempted to discover the one principle of the world.

If you look at the world as it presents itself to us, it is clearly diverse (many). The question is how do we reconcile the one principle with plurality and change? We find in the world the problem of the one and the many, unity in diversity or identity in difference.

The Pythagoreans asserted plurality to the exclusion of the ONE. The Eleatics asserted the ONE to the exclusion of the many. If you cling to plurality which is supported by sense experience, then you admit change, and if you admit change of one thing into another, you cannot avoid the endemic problem as to the character of a discernible common element in the things that change. If you start and affirm the doctrine of the one, you must deduce plurality from the one or at least show how the plurality, we observe in the world is consistent with the one i.e. justice must be done to the two sides, the one and the many, unity in diversity or identity in difference.

Note on Pantheism

An argument exists as to whether the ancient philosophers were pantheists.
1. If a pantheist is a man who has a subjective religious attitude towards the universe which he identifies with God, the Pre-Socratics are scarcely to be regarded as pantheists. All of them

spoke of the one but none overtly adopted any religious attitude towards the one.

2. If a pantheist is a man, while denying a transcendent principle of the universe, makes the universe to be ultimately thought unlike the materialist, who makes it matter alone, then again the Pre-Socratics scarcely merit the name pantheists, for they spoke of the 'one' in material terms. Rather than call them Pantheists, it is decidedly preferable to call them monists (COPLESTON 1967, 55-59).

The Pluralists

2.   Empedocles of Acragas 493 – 433BC
He was born in Sicily in South Italy. He did not produce any new philosophy but in an eclectic manner welded together and reconciled the thoughts of his predecessors. He was the first of the pluralists about whom we know something. He shared the view of Parmenides that nothing is either created or destroyed but he disagreed with Parmenides' view of the impossibility of motion. It must be noted that Parmenides thought that because there is nothing, that there could be no void, that reality must be completely full without empty spaces. Empedocles in his own way sought to reconcile this Parmenidean view with common sense experience. Parmenides had said that motion and monism are contradictory but Empedocles went ahead to agree with Parmenides while at the same time saying that if motion and monism are contradictory, that motion and pluralism cannot at the same time be contradictory. In this way, Empedocles saw reality as plurality. He said that "the many that make up reality are capable of motion but not movement into empty space but the kind of movement whereby one of the many takes the place of some other one of the many".

Empedocles made a giant stride in his explanation of the possibility of motion. Taking reality to be plurality, he showed that motion is possible contrary to the views of Parmenides and Zeno. He said that reality does not allow vacuum as could be found in the experiment of dipping one end of a tube into water and at the same time using a finger to close the other end. Here water will not enter the tube because air occupies all the available space in the tube but as soon as the finger is removed, the air will leave the tube while the space is simultaneously occupied by water. But note that water and air is not unity; instead they are different plural things in the world. So motion is possible if plurality is the order. Hence motion in a plenum is possible provided that reality is a plurality and not a unity. But Parmenides held that reality is unity and therefore motion is impossible. It is clear here that Empedocles has given us the many that moves, as against the Parmenidean unity that is immobile.

World Process

He began his explanation by enunciating what he termed the four roots. In the fashion of the Ionians, Empedocles seeks the ultimate basis of things and declares it to be four fold i.e. fire, water, earth and boundless Air. These four elements are not produced by anything else, they have no origin but they are the absolutely basic constituent of things. Empedocles calls these elements the roots of all. Earth cannot become water or water, Earth. These four kinds of matter are unchangeable and are the ultimate particles which form the complete objects of the world.

In explaining cosmic process, Empedocles started by postulating an active force. These forces he found in the twin elements of love and hate or harmony and discord. Love he defined as the motion that unites all things thereby forming a mixture while hate or strife is that, that separates the mixture into its component parts. The world process as Empedocles conceived it is a continuous cyclical process. Under the influence of these two opposites i.e. love and strife, the successive union and separation of the four basic elements take place. Union and separation never cease their continuous exchange. Sometimes uniting under the influence of love so that all of them become the ONE. At other times, each move apart through the hostile force of Hate, in the course of this process, the different characteristics of the four elements become successively predominant, each has its own character and they prevail in turn in the course of time. The active force of love brings the particles together and builds them up. It also follows that hate will be responsible for their separation.

According to Empedocles, world process is circular and we have periodic world cycles. At the commencement of the circle, the elements all mix up together i.e. a general mixture of the particles, Air, Water, Earth and Fire. In this primary state, love is the governing principle, hate or discord is however around the corner, when it permeates within its sphere, the process of separation, the disuniting of the four elements is begun until the separation becomes complete. Hate reigns supreme, then, Love having been driven out. Yet Love around the corner in turn begins its work and so causes gradual uniting and mingling of the four elements. It is then again the turn of hate to start anew. Empedocles tells us that this process continues without first beginning and without last ending. According to Empedocles, it is the alternating domination of love and hate that explains the world process.

In conclusion, it will be worthy to mention that Empedocles tried to reconcile the thesis of Parmenides that we can neither come to be nor pass away with the evident fact of change by postulating ultimate particles of the four elements the mingling mixture of which forms the concrete objects of this world and the separation of which constitute the passing away of substances.

Criticisms

From strict philosophy, Empedocles offers very little that can be called autochthonous or original and profound. He only popularized the doctrine already worked out by the preceding philosophers. His introduction of the metaphorical forces of love and hate are introduced to salvage him from the pit of confusion which he fell into. This explains why Aristotle describes Empedocles as an example of "those who having nothing to say, yet pretend to say something". In the four elements he stereotyped the basic opposites of the Ionians in such a way that the doctrine attains lasting appeal and becomes known as the Empedoclean elements. Empedocles in his motive to find explanation to the problems of the one and the many wandered off the track by positing the many as the real stuff instead of the traditional one basic ultimate stuff. He could not draw a dichotomy between monism and pluralism.

3. Anaxagoras of Clazomenae 500 – 428 BC

Although he lived in Clazomenae, he was an Ionian. He was a friend of Pericles and a dominant figure of the Periclean School. Pericles was a pupil of Anaxagoras.

Like Empedocles, Anaxagoras supported the theory of Parmenides "that nothing comes to be or passes away". For Anaxagoras "all things were together, unlimited both in number and smallness; for the small too was unlimited. When all was together none was visible on account of their smallness" (OWENS 1959, 115). Being is unchangeable. He was Empedocles first critic. He does not agree with Empedocles that the ultimate units are particles corresponding with the four elements. Anaxagoras asked the "how" question relating to the views of Empedocles. He asked: how can the union of the Empedoclean elements give rise to the things in the world like Lion, Goat, Chairs, etc. He started by asking "how can hair come from what is not hair or flesh from what is not flesh". To this extent, it could be said that Anaxagoras agreed with Parmenides that change of one thing into another thing is an illusion.

Personal Mannerism

Anaxagoras in his own idiosyncrasy felt that it will be pertinent to solve the problem of reality by distinguishing between the worlds of appearance as the senses reveal to us and the world of reality as reason reveals to us.

He started to tackle these problems on the following assumptions:

1. That the stuff of the world is eternal
2. That there is a many, each of which is a Parmenidean one
3. That there is motion i.e. change of relative spatial position of the parts of a plenum

When these presuppositions are carefully and profoundly looked into, one would find that they are in consonance with those of Empedocles. According to Anaxagoras, Empedocles fell into an avoidable contradiction by holding that things can change and still remain the same. To Anaxagoras, nothing comes into being or passes away, all we have are all there are therefore sense objects must result from "a mingling and separation of things that are". He asks "How can the qualitatively unchanging many become the changing many of the sense world?" Note that Empedocles regarded his four elements i.e. the many as unchanging i.e. as the root and again that they are responsible for the different things we see in the world. To avoid falling into a similar pit, Anaxagoras postulated that what the world process really is, is that everything in the world are mixtures of every other thing in the world but names are ascribed to things depending on the stuff that dominates the mixture. For example, what we call hair is a mixture of every other thing like lion stuff, goat stuff, cabbage stuff, flesh stuff but it is called hair because hair stuff dominates the mixture. In the same way what we call flesh is a composition of all other stuffs but with flesh as the predominant stuff. The problem of not noticing the presence of other stuffs is attributable to the fact that our sense as a source of knowledge is grossly inadequate. Anaxagoras therefore replaced the Empedoclean four roots with an infinite diversity of qualitatively different seeds or stuffs.

Anaxagoras teaches that "everything which has parts qualitatively the same as the whole is ultimate and underived". Suppose that a piece of Gold is cut into half, the halves are themselves Gold. The same thing happens to an orange. But in the case of a living thing like dog, if a dog is cut into two, the halves are not dogs anymore although they are not both living things but the constituents of the parts remain the same qualitatively. Anaxagoras did not take the four roots of Empedocles as the ultimate stuff but regarded them as mixtures composed of many qualitatively different particles.

Anaxagoras is quoted as saying that "All things were together, infinite both in number and in smallness; for the small too was infinite. And, when all things were together, none of them could be distinguished for their smallness. All things are in the whole". The objects of experience arise, when the mixture is such that certain stuffs Predominate.

Anaxagoras is said to have said that "there is a portion of everything is everything" and that the things in the world are not divided nor cut off from one another with a hatchet, neither the warm form the cold nor the cold from the warm". By this he means that there is complete mixture which does not allow us to dictate which particle is which in the mixture except that names are assigned to a given mixture depending on the stuff that predominates. It should be noted that Anaxagoras sought to maintain the Parmenidean doctrine concerning being i.e. that being is one and at the same time adopting a realist attitude towards change. He did not dismiss change as a sort of phantasmagoria (illusion) but tried to act as a mediator between the evident fact of change and the Parmenidean doctrine of the one.

As regards to the process of mixture of these stuffs in various proportions, Anaxagoras replaced Empedocles' love and strife with a single notion "mind". With Anaxagoras we enter into a different speculation. He identified a living force called "Nous" and this has been translated by those who read and understand Greek as mind or intelligence. Anaxagoras is the first Greek philosopher to use Nous. Nous "is infinite and self ruled, and is mixed with nothing but is alone, itself by itself" Anaxagoras says that Nous is different from the mass of elementary bodies that it moves. Nous pervades the whole universe. It is the source of ordered motion. He described Nous as "the finest of all things and the purest, and it has all knowledge about everything and the greatest power. Nous is everywhere in the mixture but at the same time cannot be identified with the mixture" (COPLESTON 1967, 70). According to Anaxagoras, Nous is the directing and moving force in the whole process of the ordered formation of the universe. He says that in a complete mixture, that the Nous or mind enters and sets the mixture into circular motion causing the various or different stuffs to separate off. According to him, it is the activity of separating off caused by the mind that gives rise to stars, sun, moon, air, the separation off of the rare and the dense, the warm from the cold, the light from the dark and the dry from the moist.

His doctrine leads him to affirm that since there are seeds of every kind of stuff in every sensible thing, that there must be an infinite number of seeds and it follows according to him that the seeds must be infinitely small otherwise there will be no room for all stuffs to participate in an object of small magnitude like a grain of sand.

Anaxagoras explained sensation by saying that we experience heat, cold, light, dark, etc., and other sensible qualities by the presence in us of their opposites. The hot in us is cold; the cold in us is heated by contact with the hot external object. Sensation therefore goes by contraries.

Empedocles and Anaxagoras have not solved the problem instead they have helped to formulate it more clearly. The question now is, how can we get to the world of various sense things from qualitatively single but quantitatively plural things or vice versa? Empedocles and Anaxagoras did set in motion the conception of a mechanical universe.

Anaxagoras' invention of the nous which he gave material attributes of being finite and corporeal, is not in consonance with the modern known attribute of mind which nous stands for. Again the question of the Nous being in the mixture without being involved or a part of the mixture is still confusing. Although there is a possibility of a thing exerting influence from a distance but in the case of Anaxagoras' Nous, one is tended to see it as playing a role which cannot permit it to operate without being really involved. The explanation of the Nous is not clear enough but could be regarded as a postulated concept which was brought in to free Anaxagoras from the quagmire in which he found himself. Anaxagoras philosophy also has the pitfall of, in a subtle manner discarding the monism of the earlier Ionians and the giving of pluralism a more elevated status.

He could not rise beyond materialism hence his description of Nous in materialistic terms. His concept of the Nous influenced the scholastic philosophers like Aquinas, St Augustine, Anselem, etc.

The Later Pluralists
The Atomists

Atomism is the final development of pluralism. The atomists are Leucippus, Democritus, Epicurus and Lucretius. Among the atomists, Democritus and Epicurus have their copious works still extant. But the most influential in this school of philosophy are Democritus and Leucippus.

Leucippus of Miletus is acclaimed the founder of the atomist school. But his life is still shrouded in obscurity and this has led some people to claim that he never existed. His dates cannot be fixed. However, Aristotle and Theophrastus emphasize that Leucippus was a member of the School of Parmenides and a disciple of Zeno. They claim that he actually existed as can be seen in the book Diogenes' Life of Leucippus (COPLESTON 1967, 72). But in order not to fritter away our energy on Leucippus whose contributions are not quantifiable due to the uncertainty surrounding his existence; we shall direct our attention to Democritus who is a worthy representative of the atomist school. But it should be noted that since Democritus existed at a later date, one cannot with accuracy and certainty determine the doctrines that were propounded by Democritus and that presented by his master Leucippus. To some extent, in treating Democritus, one is as well lumping together the views of a master and a pupil without clear demarcation. But since Democritus left copious works to his credit, it is only fair that we should regard him as the purveyor of the basic tenets of atomism. Again, there is some historical confusion as to the period to which to put Democritus. But according to most authors, Democritus could be classed among the Pre-Socratics. Copleston thinks otherwise (COPLESTON 1967, 72).

Democritus of Abdera is said to have lived between 494-404BC. The atomist philosophy is regarded as the logical development of the doctrine of Empedocles. It should be remembered that Empedocles in his explanation of the world process, agreed with Parmenides in the impossibility of the coming into existence and passing away of being. But with the evident fact of change, he posited the four elements i.e. Water, Air, Earth and Fire as the root of all things. These elements mixed in various proportions to give rise to the multitude of things that exist in the world. In giving his explanation he did not really work out his doctrines of particles and in the same vein did not carry the quantitative explanation of qualitative differences to its logical conclusion. The philosophy of Empedocles formed a transitional stage to the explanation of all qualitative differences by a mechanical juxtaposition of material particles in various patterns. In the universe we have diverse things each of which differs quantitatively and qualitatively. But to resolve these qualitative differences, Empedocles tried to give a quantitative explanation by saying that the proportion of the mixture of the four elements is responsible for the qualitative difference thereby positing a finite qualitative diversity as against Anaxagoras infinite qualitative diversity. Empedocles, did not in a quantitative sense tell us what these elements consist of, the real mechanism that is involved before the diverse sensible things are formed. Again the introduction of the metaphorical forces of love and hate in the philosophy of Empedocles is not in consonance with a thorough-going and efficacious mechanical philosophy. It was in effort to achieve a complete mechanical philosophy that the atomists came to be regarded.

     In the atomist philosophy, their starting point is that there is infinite number of indivisible units called atoms which exist in the universe. According to them, all there are in the world are atoms and void. Democritus says that these atoms are imperceptible i.e. that they cannot be perceived by the senses. And that they are indivisible because they are too small. They have no quality except that of impenetrability and solidity. They differ in their shape and size. They move randomly in void. The atoms of the atomists are indistinguishable. The atomists posited a many each one of which is eternal, indestructible, uncreated and indivisible. To enable the atoms of the atomists to make movement, Democritus was propelled by necessity to posit the existence of space or void to enable his atoms to exercise some movement. It must be remembered that Parmenides in his bid to be logically consistent, denied the existence of space which he classified as not-being. But when it was Pythagoras turn, he admitted the existence of void to keep his units apart. Democritus admitted the reality of space because as he said, Parmenides instead of conceiving space as something perceived it as nothing. The atomists in a different way evolved a new conception of space as something and according to them if space is something it must of necessity exist. This led the atomists to divide reality into empty and full. Things in the world i.e. atoms consist of the full reality while spaces consist of empty reality.

In respect to the motion of atoms, Democritus held that atoms are eternally conditioned to move in a random manner like the motes or particles in the sun beam. That these atoms dart about in the void in all directions even when there is no wind. Here one finds that Democritus tactfully avoided explaining the source of motion of the atoms. He did not want to fall into the disrepute of Empedocles and Anaxagoras who had to bring in the metaphorical concepts of love and hate and the 'Nous' respectively to explain the cause of motion. The motion of the atomists is the change of place and not that of older Greek philosopher Thales who posited the change of one substance into another e.g. water giving rise to wind, fire, earth, etc. The metaphorical concepts of the early pluralists were introduced as a drowning-man's measure to explain the world process. In avoidance of falling into the same temptation, Democritus asserted that the movement of atoms is eternal and needs no further explanation.

To explain the world process, Democritus held that as the atoms dart about in the void, that collisions occur and in the course of these collisions, atoms with irregular shapes link up with one another forming a chain of atoms and in this way a vortex is set up and configuration of objects take place hence forming the different sensible things in the world. He says "in this way the numerable worlds arise from the collisions among the infinite atoms moving in the void". Human soul and the gods are said to be fine atoms linked up together. The atoms are each the Parmenidean one and collectively make up the many—this is an explanation of how the many comes out of the one.

Some people have suggested that Democritus could be regarded as a sophist following his saying that "man is cut off from truth; and that in truth we know nothing about anything, but every man shares the generally prevailing opinion". But in another fragment, Democritus distinguishes between two forms of knowledge, the genuine knowledge and the bastard or obscure knowledge. The sight, hearing, smell, taste and feeling belong to the obscure while thought (reason) leads us to genuine knowledge. With this, far from being a sophist, he believed that the human mind is capable of understanding the world. He held that there is an objective public world that can be discovered by reason.

From the foregoing, the atomists could be regarded as having taken the tendencies of preceding philosophers to their logical conclusion. Presenting a purely mechanical account of reality. They gave the account of the universe in terms of mechanical materialism. The atomist's theory is important in physics and really influenced subsequent scientists. Atomism could therefore be viewed as a concerted attempt to solve the dilemma of change and the problem of the one and the many.

His Ethics or Moral Wisdom
The ethical system of Democritus was the first example of the type that was to become very common later. The atomists could be said to have launched us into another sphere, that of Ethics. The fact that they were interested in Ethics at all and had morality to teach shows that we are now clearly in a new epoch of philosophy. We are now passing from the world of thought of the pre-Socratic's with the almost exclusive cosmological preoccupation to that of Socrates and his contemporaries with their concern about the good life of man and the proper end of life. With Democritus the traditional Greek moral wisdom of self knowledge and moderation is made to

bear upon living cheerfully. He is quoted as saying that "He who is to be of good cheer must not undertake a multitude of activities either in private or public life and in those that he would undertake, he must not choose things above his own strength and natural capacity, but he must be sufficient on his guide both to set aside any stroke of fortune coming his way and leading him to excess through appearance and not to meddle with things beyond his powers, moderate bulk is safer than massive bulk". To him, cheerfulness is the goal towards which ones private and public life should be directed.

Democritus was concerned with the goodness of the soul than the body. As he says "if one chooses the goods of the soul, he chooses the diviner portion, if the goods of the body, the merely mortal". He envisages wisdom doing for the soul what medicine does for the body. "Medical science cures diseases of the body, but wisdom rids the soul of passion". He says that happiness is derived from uprightness and in fullness of understanding. To him, one should refrain from doing wrong not because of fear of the repercussion but from a sense of duty.

He who does wrong is unhappy than he who suffers wrong. According to him, "tranquility can only be achieved through moderation in pleasure and through symmetry of life" (i.e. through harmony). He was chiefly concerned with practical rather than theoretical wisdom. He was concerned with formulating a recipe for a good life.

Shortcomings of Atomism
1. The denial of the existence of a primal cause of motion: They did not explain the source and kind of motion. The question which they have to answer is "is the movement of atoms borne out of chance?" In the world we know that things do not happen by chance at least not all things. There is a discernible order which seems to follow natural laws. We cannot be contented with admitting that the universe came to be through the chance collision of atoms.

2.   Since the atoms can be likened to the Pythagorean units, then they also have the pitfall of being pluralistic i.e. deviating from the monistic tradition of the early Greek thinkers like Thales.
3.   Their explanation of the existence of innumerable things as a resultant effect of the interplay of atoms is not completely plausible. Why has the interplay seemed to have stopped? Why are more things not arising out of the interplay of atoms now? It is contrary to reason to suppose that the interplay of atoms caused the multitude of things in the world. It is preposterous to hold that there is no law governing the universe.

But, all in all, atomism marks a continued development of the inquiry which began with Thales

Pre-Socratic Philosophy in Retrospect

Here an attempt is being made to give a conspectus of the philosophy that preceded Socratic period. Greek philosophy at the time we are talking about centered on the problem of the one and the many. The notion of unity was also articulated. They believed that things change into one another. Therefore there must be some common substratum, some ultimate principle or unity underlying the diversity. Thales declared water as the principle, for Anaximenes it was air, Heraclitus fire, etc. All of them chose different principles but all believed in one ultimate principle. As far as strict scientific proof goes, they have no sufficient data to warrant their assertion of unity but at least all of them believed that everything is one. But if we look at their work from a strict scientific perspective, we will see that they lacked enough empirical data to support their claims although some of the things they said remained valid up till now.

They were all fascinated by the idea of cosmic unity. They were faced with the fact of the many and they had to attempt conceptual reconciliation of the evident plurality with the postulated unity, i.e. they tried to give account of the world as we know it. In trying to do this we ought to remember that contrary to sense experience, that Parmenides held his being to be one and changeless. Anaximander held that his first principle was the unlimited. While they battled with the problem of the one and the many, they did not succeed in solving it. It was rather left to be borne by Aristotle and Plato who had used their talent and ingenuity to offer their own solutions.

The Pre-Socratics were also cosmologists because they were concerned with the nature of the universe. Man was also regarded as an objective item in the cosmos rather than regarding him as a subjective item. In their account of the cosmos, they had no definite conclusion for all the facts involved. This failure coupled with other factors led to a change of interest from objects i.e. cosmos to subject man. The change of interest we will find exemplified in the sophists.

Although we have said all these things, man himself was not completely neglected in pre-Socratic philosophy. The notion between sense experience and reason was raised by no other than Parmenides.

The early Greek thinkers justly qualified to be termed philosophers since they proceeded largely by way of action and reaction, of thesis and anti thesis i.e. Heraclitus overemphasizing becoming and Parmenides overstressing Being. It was only to be expected that the gems of later philosophical tendencies and schools were already discernible in Pre-Socratic philosophy e.g. in Anaxagoras we have the gems of philosophical theism. From atomism we have the gems of later materialistic and mechanistic philosophy i.e. reducing everything in the universe to matter.

From all these, it can be seen easily that the Pre-Socratic philosophy was not simply a pre- philosophical period but that it is the very first stage of Greek philosophy. It may not have been very pure but it was philosophy and still is philosophy hence it is absurd to start Greek philosophy from Plato, Aristotle and others who were undoubtedly influenced by the Pre-Socratic philosophers. Also the knowledge of the present cannot even make sense without the knowledge of the past (See COPLESTON 1967, 76-80).

CHAPTER TEN

THE SOPHISTS

Background

The earlier Greek philosophers concerned themselves with finding an objective truth to explain the composition of the universe. They therefore directed their attention to the subject i.e. universe but when the Sophists came, they deviated from the cosmological inquiry of the early Greek philosophers and focused their attention on man. This in effect marks a change from the macrocosm to the microcosm. The earlier philosophers raised problems which they attempted to solve without success. The Sophists being aware of the impossibility of attaining an objective truth about the universe because of the untrustworthy nature of our senses sought to direct their energies towards the study of the nature of man, his culture, society, etc., the bankruptcy and futility of the search of early cosmologists discouraged them from pursuing the search to its conclusion, although Plato and Aristotle lent a hand by attempting to find solutions to these problems raised by the cosmologists.

The Sophists indulged in a rational and enthusiastic reflection on the disparity in the cultures and civilizations of different societies. At this period, the Greeks were in contact with foreign peoples like the Persians, the Babylonians, the Thracians, the Egyptians, etc. The discernible differences in the culture, and civilizations of these different peoples, made the Greeks (Sophists) to ask questions like "Are the various national and local ways of life, religious and ethical codes merely conventions or not"? Also they wanted to know whether there are immutable and common characteristics belonging to all cultures or whether they are products of individual societies. But having viewed the different cultures, they came up with the discovery that there are no divine sanctions imposed on any culture and that cultures differ from society to society. To them therefore customs, civilizations, and cultures are relative.

The Sophists changed the traditional object of inquiry into that of man because at this time man was becoming more self conscious and wanted to know more about himself as is borne out of the quotation of Sophocles that "Miracles in the world are many, there is no greater miracle than man". Sophism differed from the older Greek philosophy in many other respects. While the method of Early Greek philosophy did not exclude empirical observation but was mainly deductive, the method of Sophism starts by examining the different particulars and drawing conclusions therefrom. Their method is therefore Empirico-inductive. Their conclusions were partly practical and partly theoretical. For example, from the store of facts accumulated on the differences of opinion and belief, they might conclude that it is impossible to have certain knowledge. Unlike the early Greek philosophers, the Sophists were not interested in establishing objective truths but in practical things.

Sophism later became an instrument of instruction and teaching in the Greek city state. And their aim was to teach the art and meaning of life. They were itinerant teachers who travelled from city to city instructing and teaching in various themes, grammar, interpretation of poems, Religion, etc.

The Sophists inculcated talents of facility in debate and oratorical skill. They taught virtue and this encompasses teaching techniques that engenders success in the new Athenian democracy. Though the Sophists did not all teach the same thing, but they were united by their common aspiration to subdue the existing Greek tradition of their time. Since they felt themselves enlightened they thought themselves as having been liberated from the stupor of ignorance and superstition and in effect directed their energies towards the liberation of other less fortunate citizens. Note that at this period that the old education was regarded as insufficient for the man who wished to make his mark in the state. The aristocratic ideals of the old were at this time outmoded and no longer met the needs of the democratic period. Plutarch says that the Sophists put a theoretical training in the place of the older practical training which was largely an affair of family tradition and actual practical and experiential training by actual participation in political life.

These itinerant encyclopedists taught the art of rhetoric which was absolutely necessary in Greek political life. At this time, no one can aspire to any public office unless he could speak well. The sophists professed to teach the youth how to do so. They also taught Eristic i.e. teaching the right way of winning law suits. The youth were their most ardent pupils. This made heads of tradition to regard sophism with suspicion. The Sophists were accused of gathering the youths and pulling down to pieces before them the traditional ethical code and religious beliefs hitherto prevalent in Greece. The Sophists took money for teaching their pupils. Although this practice was legitimate it was at variance with the tradition of the earlier philosophers. The relativistic posture of the Sophists led to skepticism i.e. that we cannot know any thing because of the gross inadequacy of our senses. They were regarded as charlatans by the preservers of the status quo. Sophism serves as a transition stage to the great Platonic and Aristotelian achievements. Plato is our source of information about the Sophists. This source is not proper since Plato himself was a prejudiced observer. Sophism does not deserve outright condemnation because by turning attention to man himself, Sophism has widened the scope of our inquiry. Sophism also raised its own problems which were left to Plato and Aristotle to settle.

1.   Protagoras of Abdera

Protagoras is a native of Abdera in Thrace. Most authors put his date at 481 but Plato and Burnet are of the view that he was born much earlier i.e. about 500BC.

Of the words attributed to Protagoras, only two fragments of philosophical importance have been preserved. The first sets up man as the measure of things.

a.   Man as a Measure

The best known saying of Protagoras is that contained in his work which says that "man is the measure of all things, of the things that are, that they are, and of the things that are not, that they are not". There has been a controversy as to how his statement could be interpreted. Different people have interpreted it in various ways. Some writers hold that Protagoras by man means the individual man while others argue that man is viewed in a specific sense. Looking at the two views i.e. whether man is viewed as a community or group of men or whether man is viewed as individual one will still make something meaningful out of this dictum of Protagoras. In the world we know that different societies have different cultures and also that different individual people perceive things differently. Plato admits that the dictum could be interpreted in individualistic sense in regard to sense perception.

Socrates observes that when the same wind is blowing, that one person may feel chilly while another does not. He asks does this mean that the wind is both chilly and not chilly at the same time. He answers that the individuals perceive the same thing differently depending on their dispositions. But Protagoras would say that both the person who says that the wind is chilly and the other who does not believe so are correct when the phenomena are examined in respect to their sense organs.

In regard to ethical values and judgments, Protagoras held that they are relative. He says that "for I hold that whatever practices seem right and laudable to any particular state are so for that state, so long as it holds for them". According to him "there is no question of one ethical view being true and another being false, but there is question of one view being sounder" i.e. more useful or expedient than another. In other words, one can say that Protagoras gave opinion the status of truth.

The popular dictum of Protagoras that "man is a measure" has an Eleatic flavor because it could be used to explain Being and not-Being. This means that man is the measure of both Being and not-Being. This follows that it is man that gives the picture of what is i.e. Being and appearance i.e. Not Being. Protagoras therefore, reduces all human knowledge to opinion.

b. Knowledge about the Gods

Another fragment that is of philosophical interest reads "about the gods I have no way of knowing either whether they exist or they do not exist nor what kind they are in form, for many are the things that hinder knowledge, the obscurity of the subject and the fact that the life of man is short" what this quotation is suggesting is that since we cannot understand the nature of the gods, that we ought to follow the traditional religion of our fathers. Another interpretation that could be given is that since objective truth is impossible, that we should discard the search for this kind of truth and be content with knowledge of the senses. He says that since logic and reason force us to uphold the authenticity of an elusive reality as Parmenides held, that it will be better to take as real the reality of what we see and operate on that basis.

Dialectics

Protagoras is credited as being the first to say that there are two contradictory accounts about every thing. Men construct their appearances out of two contradictory forms, hence mutually contradictory aspects can be found and developed in all constructions e.g. it is possible that God is existing and its negation is possible also.

Protagoras is said to be a pioneer in the study and science of grammar. He is said to have classified the different kinds of sentence and to have distinguished terminologically the genders of nouns (COPLESTON 1967, 81-91).

Evaluation

From Protagoras we learn that truth is relative, that human sensation and cognition are relative. Protagoras worked out a theory of sense perception based on Heraclitean physical theory. Heraclitus had held that everything is in a state of flux in the same way Protagoras held that there is no stability or immutability in knowledge that what we have are opinions which differ from person to person, from society to society. He says that since neither reason nor sense perception gives us true knowledge about the world, that it follows that objective knowledge of a public reality is impossible.

When we say that truth, sensation, etc., are relative, is value relative what do we mean? Are there human values valid to all human beings at all times? To Protagoras justice/injustice, good or bad are not absolutely valid principles. Note that from Thales, that objective truth or reality had been affirmed as a possibility but Protagoras discarded this view. The consequences of holding a wholly relative view of reality can be very damaging from the epistemological point of view. In integrative humanism we hold that some things can be known objectively and others can be known relatively and yet others can be known to be absolutely the case within the context of contextuality. For instance, I know that I have two hands with absolute certainty within the context of human perception. But when it comes to what we believe, people can believe different things (see OZUMBA and CHIMAKONAM 2014, 33-54).

2. Thrasymachus

Plato presents Thrasymachus in his Republic as a sophist who became popular for arguing that injustice pays better than justice. An unjust man can do anything to achieve the goal he has set for himself. The just man in his attempt to be just will not be able to adopt unscrupulous means to achieve his aim. Eventually he fails to achieve his aim and is counted a failure. Thrasymachus it seems will agree with Machiavelli that it is the end that justifies the means.

He further goes on to say that might is right and justice is the interest of the stronger party. This means that it is the strong that should dictate what is right. Or, the just and the weak should be made to submit willy nilly. This, he says is the case in all systems of government. Even in a democracy, it is still the strong elected representatives who make laws and it is the strong executives who execute the laws and the strong in the judiciary who interpret the law. This shows that the weak has no say in how he is governed. Even his only weapon which is his vote is also neutralized through rigging. This is why it has become legitimate in irrational politics to permit any invidious means as legitimate. However, is important to say that what is presently the case is not in accord with the ought. The ought is the ideal, the right thing. As such nations must do everything possible to destroy the bases for Thrasymachianism and Machiavellianism in our body-politic.

3.   **Gorgias of Leontini 483-375 B.C**
He was a successful teacher of rhetoric and was a pupil of Empedocles. His main work in Philosophy is called "On not Being or On Nature". He was led to skepticism by the dialectics of Zeno. Unlike Protagoras he reacted differently to the Eleatic philosophy. Protagoras in his own case regarded every opinion as true but in the case of Gorgias he held every opinion as false. We gather the works of Gorgias from Sextus Empiricus and from pseudo-Aristotelian writings on Melissus, Xenophanes and Gorgias. His argument aimed at establishing three assertions.
1.   Nothing is (nothing exists, there is nothing)
2.   Even if anything is, it is unknowable to man
3.   Even if anything is knowable, it is inexpressible and incommunicable to others therefore, nothing is (nothing exists)

Nothing is (nothing exists)
The first assertion is established by a dialectic that is based upon the Eleatic philosophy. If anything is, it will be either Being or not-Being or both Being and not- Being. It cannot be Not-Being and Being combined this is so because it is self contradictory to say that "Not Being is" and "Being which is its opposite is". He goes further to say that Being cannot be because for it to be it must either be eternal or to have come into being or both. But it could not have come into being, for neither out of Being not out of Not-Being can anything come to be. What is is and cannot give rise to another thing and what is not is not and cannot give rise to what is. Again, it cannot be eternal for if it were eternal, then it would have to be infinite i.e. without limit and as unlimited; it would have no where to exist and so will not be at all. It cannot be both eternal and

something that has come into Being because each of those characteristics cancels out the other. If not Being is not existing then Not-Being will be no less than Being. In this way Being is shown to be identical with Not-Being and since Not-Being is not, therefore Being which is identical with it likewise is not. Moreover, if it is, it is either one or many. It cannot be one because it is extended and so is divisible and composed of plurality but if in this way there is no unit it cannot be many because plurality is composed of units nor could it move because change would mean that "Is" cease to "Be" and what is not comes into Being and besides motion would required a void and void is nothing and nothing cannot be. This is a kind of circumlocution of argument which is logically valid.

Second argument -in Relation to Second Assertion

Even if anything is, it is unknowable for Being is not a property of things thought. One can think of a chariot running over the sea, of a chimera, of a mirage or of other things that have no being. Each sense attains its own object and only its own object. If Being were a characteristic of things thought, one would have to say that anything thought is, even though it is not perceived by any of the senses. Being therefore is not attained by thought and is not an object of thought. Being is unknowable. This argument admits the presence of sensible things while denying to human cognition the power of recognizing any Being in them.

Third Argument

Even if Beings could be known, they could not be expressed in speech or communicated to others. Speech is different from beings, if by beings are meant the sensible things in the outside world. But speed is not one of the sensible things therefore it is only the speed itself that is communicated and not the Beings. Just as the objects of various senses are different from one another, so are they different from our speech and as they differ in each individual and from moment to moment in the same individual, they provide no object that could remain the same when communicated from one person to another. This view presupposes the flux of Heraclitus.

Again, this argument supposes the presence of sensible things in the outside world. The argument takes or granted that if being is to be found any where, it is to be located in those sensible things. Though sensible things are different from speech and so cannot be expressed or conveyed by speech, they are in a continual flux, moreover they do not exhibit the sameness that would be required for the communication of a thing from one individual to another individual. Parmenides maintained that Not-Being is neither knowable nor expressible. Gorgias against the background of the Eleatics has shown the same of Being. The arguments of the inability of one's sense to attain the object of another seem to indicate the influence of Empedocles' doctrine of sensation and the relativity of the objects of sensation is in full agreement with the Parmenidean world of appearances and more as reflected in the cognitional tenets of Protagoras. The nature dealt with by the treatise of Gorgias which consists of a universe of sensible flux coincides with illusory world of seeming of Parmenides.

Peoples' Various Reactions to the Philosophy of Gorgias
What is the exact bearing of the long argument of Gorgias?

His reasoning has been interpreted in various ways by historians and philosophers. By some, the argument has been regarded as a display of Gorgias rhetorical ability to prove anything even the most absurd. By some, it is looked upon as a parody of eleatic reasoning. Yet others regard it as attack on all the preceding Greek philosophers.

In a more positive fashion, it has been interpreted as the tragic view of human life, extended now to human thought or as an effort leading up to the abolition of the Copula (is) in regard to the phenomenal objects on account of the contradictions that the Copula 'is' involves.

The later interpretation is supported by Aristotle's correction that Gorgias and his disciples wished to remove the verb 'is' from speech. Socrates, Gorgias' own pupil understood him to mean "that there really is nothing". These consideration makes it difficult to take the reasoning in any other sense than as meant to prove that there actually are no beings in the world. The concept of Being that his argument presumes includes what in English language is called real existence but also involves the aspect of something absolutely unchangeable.

If either of these characteristics is lacking, the notion of being is destroyed. Accordingly, both notions i.e. real existence and absolute unchangeableness are necessary for the conception of Being. Gorgias seriously wished to remove the aspect of Being understood in the foregoing eleatic way in the world in which man lives and acts. If the caption 'On not Being or On Nature" was meant as a single title, it implies that the world of nature is a world of not-Being. This is a world that cannot be understood or explained in terms of Being. Its components reveal themselves as sensible things but not as being.

The Sophists as seen by later Philosophers

The term sophist had the original meaning of a skilled craftsman or artist. It was applied to musicians, poets and to experts in the various crafts. Later, it was used to describe anyone who was eminent for knowledge whether theoretical or practical. It came to be associated with any person who has devoted himself to the pursuit of wisdom. In the fifth century, it came to be attributed to those who make a profession out of teaching their own brand of wisdom. They were itinerant teachers who traveled from place to place teaching people for a fee.

The Sophists capitalized on the fashion of their time which necessitated ability to participate in political assemblies. During this time of direct democratic dispensation, adult freeborn were all permitted to participate in political decisions. One's fame and popularity depended on one's ability to sway public opinion to one's favour.

To excel politically, one needed the art of persuasive rhetoric and wisdom. This pursuit of political excellence is called arête. Again, the Sophists claimed to be embodiments of knowledge. They taught people "eristics" the art of winning law suits. This means teaching their students how to argue for or against any given position with convincing persuasion. This means teaching how to present cases in a convincing manner. The fashion was for the aristocrats to pay any thing to ensure that their children obtained these sophistic wares which is and believed will prepare them for future political office. This made the Sophists the first group of people to charge fees for their services. They became particularly wealthy class of people.

The Sophists according to Socrates, Plato and Aristotle were not interested in objective truth but rather make-believes and persuasive opinion. For them, truth is relative. What is more, the Sophists taught different things (on different subjects). The Sophists are said to inaugurate a new dispensation in philosophy because they were responsible for the transition of philosophy from cosmology to anthropology. They were concerned more about man and his activities in the social milieu than in "the constitution" of the universe. They were opposed to the Greek traditional beliefs and the Homeric conception of the gods. In later period, Sophism became associated with the pejorative connotation of a quibbler, that is, one who uses language in artful or clever manner to evade the point in question (that is, through prevarication).

We have considered three notable sophists namely; Protagoras of Abdera, Thrasymachus and Gorgias of Leontini and shall here present the views of Socrates, Plato and Aristotle concerning the Sophists.

Protagoras of Abdera

Protagoras is regarded as the chief Sophist; Plato described him as a masterful sophist who died at age of seventy and old enough to be the father of Socrates. He was a professional teacher who commanded high fees and he was said to have practiced this art for over forty years. He is remembered for his views that truth is relative. The same weather can be both hot and cold depending on the judgment of the individuals concerned.

His famous dictum says that "man is the measure of all things, of the things that are that they are, and of the things that are not, that they are not". Concerning the knowledge of the gods he has this to say "About the gods I have no way of knowing either whether they exist or do not exist, nor what kind they are in form, for many are the things that hinder knowledge, the obscurity of the object and the fact that the life of man is short".

Protagoras is said to be the first to hold that there are always two contrary accounts about everything. He is said to have the skill of making weaker argument appear stronger and stronger one appear weaker. Like other Sophists he taught arête, eristics and rhetoric, that is, teaching how to achieve political excellence, how to win law suits and how to make weaker account to appear stronger.

Thrasymachus

Plato presents Thrasymachus in his Republic as a Sophist who became popular for arguing that injustice pays better than justice. An unjust man can do any thing to achieve the goal he has set for himself. The just man in his attempt to be just will not be able to adopt unscrupulous means to achieve his aim. Eventually he fails to achieve his aim. Thrasymachus will appear to agree with Machiavelli that it is the end that justifies the means.

He further goes on to say that might is right and justice is the interest of the stronger party. This means that it is the strong that should dictate what is right or just and the weak should be made to submit Willy-nilly. This he says is the case in all systems of government. Even in a democracy, it is still the strong elected representatives who make laws and it is the strong executives who execute the laws and the strong in the judiciary who interpret and defend the law. The weak, the poor and those in the lower class, have little or no say. Whatever one can do to be counted among the strong is legitimate and right.

Gorgias of Leontini

Gorgias is said to have lived for more than one hundred years. He was a teacher of rhetoric. He is remembered in philosophy for his work "On not Being or On Nature". In this work he established three successive assertions namely;

(1)   that nothing exist
(2)   if there is anything it is unknowable to man
(3)   that if it is knowable, it cannot be communicated to others

Gorgias is seen as an extreme septic who denied the possibility of knowledge. He thought that nothing can be known because things are known and communicated through words and symbols. He holds that there is no one to one correspondence between symbols and what they represent. Since objects are in perpetual state of flux, it is impossible to pin them down through the use of words. This is so because before you describe them, they have changed. The question is, how then was it possible for Gorgias to communicate his own thoughts to us? A thorough going skepticism is ultimately self-defeating.

CHAPTER ELEVEN

THE GOLDEN ERA OF GREEK PHILOSOPHY I

Socrates 470-399 BC

The name of Socrates is not a hidden name in philosophy. It is hard to see how one will undertake any length of meaningful study in philosophy without coming across the name of Socrates. He begins a new epoch after the "pre-socratic" philosophers, a term coined from his name. He acts as a bridge between the early beginnings of Western philosophy and the more sophisticated era of philosophizing often called the "Golden Era" of philosophy. This era is dominated by the philosophies of the trio—Socrates, Plato and Aristotle. Socrates no doubt as the mentor and path-finder of this era provided the much needed foundation and inspiration upon which Plato and Aristotle had to recourse to for strength and intellectual ferment.

Socrates was not a mythical figure. He was born with flesh and blood; he took part in social life and even took part in soldiering. His mother was Phanarete and his father was Sophroniscus. He got married to Xantippe. His date of birth is fixed at 469 B.C. He was born in Athens, within whose walls he spent his entire life but for a few years in military service. He is said to be "Snub nosed" and ugly and became bald in later years. He was a vigorous citizen, imbued with all the endowments of courage and moral excellence. It is for these qualities that he later got into trouble with the operators of the government of the Athenian Society who were then riding on the crest of injustice and high handedness. Socrates is known for his famous dictum of "man know thyself".

a. ***The Socratic Problem***

This heading at first sight might be misleading because of the many interpretations that can be given to it. One who is not already aware of what the heading is all about, might begin to wonder the kind of problem Socrates put himself into. But the fact is that, the value of a person does not so much lie in his physical possessions but in the intellectual legacy that he has bequeathed to his generation and generations to come. This assertion is likely to be viewed with contempt and disregard except where the reader is one that has been initiated into the arts of intellectualism and the spiritual usefulness of ideas. Ideas they say rule the world. If this is true, a generation is then to be judged enlightened and knowledgeable depending on the quality and quantity of ideas they are able to generate, sustain and perpetuate to on coming generations. It is therefore in the light of the indispensability of ideas in human upliftment that we now wish to cast our deciphering light on the gamut of ideas that owe their origin in the profundity of excogitations that characterized the golden era of philosophy. It is our aim to look at the history of those ideas with a view to finding out who contributed what to the bumper harvest we have been able to make in the vineyard of knowledge. It is particularly the confusion that goes with this sifting and attribution of sets of ideas to men of this era that have generated the question of trying to find out what Socrates contributed as a person to the growth of knowledge.

It is a historical fact that, that exalted and revered Athenian wise man called Socrates, did not commit any of his ideas to paper. This means that throughout his philosophical life, he either did not find it expedient to put his thoughts on paper or was too busy propagating his ideas that he had no time left for that all important duty he owes not only his generation but future generations. This however has been seen as a great error of omission and negligence on the part of that encyclopaedic Athenian citizen. In a situation like this, what happens is that the door is thrown open for admirers and adversaries alike, to portray him in ways that please their whims and fancies. As a result, there arises a perceptual problem, since one cannot embrace any view point with the open-mindedness that is supposed to be the case. The conflicting views are bound to engender an atmosphere of uncertainty and hence bringing about half-hearted acceptance of what each narrator says. It is important that historical facts have given the stamp of consistency and truthfulness, so as to make the report authentic and of historical significance.

The "Socratic problem" then, becomes the intricacies involved in carrying out a concrete reconstruction of his views and philosophical teachings. As historians of philosophy, it is our duty to collate information and to ascertain the truth and authenticity of ideas that are attributed to great minds that have the honour of contributing their quota to the development of ideas in the world. Our duty therefore is to put the records straight and enlighten our readers about the propriety or impropriety of some of the views they find scattered all over the corpus of extant materials that are today too numerous to mention. "Of all the men of his generation whom the Athenians know as Sophists or teachers of wisdom, the most famous or notable was Socrates". He was distinguished in his perspicacity and intellectual endowments. There is a view which says that in every generation that there arises a person whose level of thinking far surpasses those of his contemporaries and who eventually dies a martyr for his far-reaching ideas and far-sightedness. Such was the position of Socrates. As a reformer he had to combat the existing prejudices and deep rooted passions of his time. In the writings of his admirers however, he was presented as a paragon of all virtues but in the eyes of his adversaries and the newly restored Athenian democracy of that time, he was seen as a "never-do-well" who was consciously corrupting the youths and subverting everything purposeful in the Athenian set up. That this later view is not true can be common-sensically dismissed because our experience show that every ruling class endeavors to entrench what are its class interests and would want every other member of the community to abide by its rules. Those found unbending in their convictions are regarded as deviants and hence a threat to the established status quo. Such reformers are rooted out fast to prevent them from spreading their "viruses" of awareness and enlightenment. Socrates was therefore a victim of these institutional machinations which outwitted him by the use of state power. He was seen as a menace to the accepted way of life, a pervertion of the traditional and moral order of Athens. These are some of the viewpoints that are expressed as to the true nature of Socrates. The fact that he did not write down anything, makes it even more difficult to state with authority and firmness the type of person one can associate with the ideas he expresses. Having discovered this loophole, people have gone forth to utilize it in presenting Socrates in diverse lights. It is in this historical lacuna that the Socratic problem takes its root. The problem has to do with finding a set of criteria for determining acceptance or rebuttal of views presented by people about Socrates. Since Socrates did not live in our time, we can only explore the abundant work on him to carefully, extract views that seem consistent within the general ambit of presentations made on him. It is only with a keen insight and unfailing dutifulness that this task can be accomplished.

We find in the literature that four main primary sources are available. These are Plato who was his direct pupil, Aristotle who in turn was Plato's pupil, Xenophon and Aristophanes who were contemporaries of Socrates. Each has presented Socrates in ways that vary widely. The difficulty of accounting for Socrates' life and thoughts, lie on the nature of the sources at our disposal. In the various sources, we find Socrates being presented in different guises that vary surprisingly. It is this that constitutes what is known as the dilemma of the Socratic philosophy.

b.   ***Reconstruction of Socrates' Philosophy***
In reconstructing the philosophy of Socrates, it is assumed that Socrates had ideas that are authochtonously his own. Also, there is that underlying but unspoken lamentation for the need to forge together all the scattered views of a man who has come to be regarded as a colossus as far as philosophical excogitations are concerned. Since the views of this man are scattered all over the gamut of extant works with different people portraying him differently, there is need to work out a systematic way of bringing together all he has said. But the difficulty which we have highlighted in the foregoing X-ray of the Socratic problem is as well relevant here. This problem, though may seem intractable, is surmountable given the will power to do so. Our perspective in this

work has been that of carrying out a general and comprehensive focus of all that have been said about Socrates. No view should be treated as being of no significance. To do this, there are bound to be a lot of valid deductions. We must move from the known to the unknown. In carrying out this reconstruction, we intend to examine the different perceptions of the four principal purveyors of Socratic history and then, attempt a synthesis of their view points and crystallize them into a coherent whole.

These principal sources are not concerned with only his philosophical teachings but his life as well. To adequately come to grips with a man's worth, his beliefs in form of teachings must not be divorced from his social life. The first source that we would want to look at is Aristophanes. He perceives Socrates as a sophist and hence identifies him with excellent capacity and skillfulness. The real setting of Aristophanes' report is in his comedy, a book called "The Cloud" which was produced in 423 B.C. In it Socrates who played the dominant role is seen as one who is the purveyor of Sophistic wares. He is seen conducting a "thinking house" or a "wisdom shop". The Cloud is a fiction in which Socrates is used to show how resourceful the sophists could be. The important fact here is that for Aristophanes to have used Socrates as the central figure in his fiction, is a pointer to show that Socrates must have been perceived in ordinary life to be doing what he was presented to be doing in "The Cloud".

In Plato's dialogues which are another source through which Socrates' philosophy can be reconstructed, we find that Plato actually was in touch with Socrates and had the privilege of hearing from the horse's mouth. He was in fact his pupil and hence has been regarded as the most viable source in reconstructing the views of his master. A lot of people have also accused him of sharing in the confusion that today surrounds the person we call Socrates. Plato would have made history straight if he had presented his master's views in very clear outline instead of muddling up his master's views with his own. This has been seen as the chief source of the problem that has engulfed historians of philosophy in the task of reconstructing Socrates' philosophy. Many have argued that

Plato lumped his views together with his master's views because he revered his master to the point of adulation. It could be said that his master overwhelmed him and completely transformed him into a "Young Socrates" which made it utterly difficult for Plato to sever his own views from that of his master. Others say that Plato consciously mixed his master's views with his as the only way of overtly paying tribute to his master. It could be that Plato saw that his master was aging and yet had not written any of his noble ideas down and hence felt that it will be a willful sin of omission if he failed to document or put down these ideals of his master which he must have seen as dazzling and inspiring.

In the Platonic dialogues therefore, we find Plato using Socrates as the mouth piece of true wisdom as well as presenting him as the embodiment of true philosophical life. The point is that we are not clear about the extent to which Socrates was used in presenting Plato's own ideas and Socrates' own ideas. It is the view of many historians of philosophy that, Plato could not have attributed to Socrates things that he never said. If this opinion is given the weight that its advocates claim, then, we can conveniently say that in the early dialogues of Plato, that Plato was merely recounting the views of his master. It could however be the case that the interlocutors of Socrates were used to put across the views of Plato himself on the issues that Socrates raised in the dialogues. This will however, conform with the authentic life history of Socrates which presents him as someone who lived by interrogating and eliciting information from people. More so, we are aware that the characters in Plato's dialogues were no mythical persons. They actually lived and in fact were contemporaries of Socrates.

Going by the information we have gathered from the dialogues of Plato, we have been made to see Socrates as the author of transcendental forms, the real theorist on the question of immortality of the soul. He was also presented as a courageous man who willingly gave up his life at the instance of the decision of the Athenian magistrates. He was presented as a teacher of moral virtue and an intellectual midwife who helped people in labour to bring to birth the ideas for which they have been heavily burdened.

Socrates was also presented as the purveyor of the real philosophical methodology which leads to the appropriation of universal standards for ascertaining knowledge. He is seen as the initiator of the view that universal definition is possible, and also that, it is through the process of dialectics that this can be realized (conversations). Having gone thus far, it becomes clear that Plato had Socrates' ideas as the fulcrum on which his own ideas had to revolve. Plato as we also know was a man of high intellectual capacity and as such it will be improper and unfair to see him as one that had no original views of his own. He must have contributed in no small measure in at least refurbishing the very austere views of his master, and if he did that, then, he as well deserves a pat on the back. No matter the position we adopt, there is no gainsaying the fact that Socrates had enormous influence on Plato, and it is in the reconstruction of these ideas that are genuinely Socratic that we can ascertain the original contributions of Socrates. We shall now look at the conception of Socrates as was presented by Xenophon.

Xenophon is another person that has actually tried to present Socrates in a way that is different from the foregoing two sources. He was a contemporary of Socrates. He was interested in the ordinary interaction of men in the Society. He was not philosophically minded and this influenced his account of the philosophy of Socrates. He presented Socrates as one who merely exercises an urban and beneficial influence on those who associate with him especially the youth. He did not present Socrates as one who concerned himself with the problems of logic and metaphysics. He saw him as an ethical teacher. Xenophon is accused of giving us a casual and peripheral account of the real nature of Socrates but could be regarded as a fair perception by a man who had little or no tincture of philosophical insight and hence could not have seen through the fog that covered the real Socrates.

In his books [The Memorabilia] and [Symposium], Socrates is presented as being the cynosure of the attention of all youth who at that time were thirsty of the wisdom that Socrates had to offer. His other books are the [Banquet] and [Apology]. He presented

Socrates the way he be-held him. The point we have to note here is that Xenophon's account informs us of the part interest and mental development play in the perception of things. Xenophon merely presented Socrates from the point of his interest. No matter the weak points of this view, it is still useful as a valuable pigeon hole through which we can look at Socrates. The last but not the least in this task of reconstructing Socrates philosophy is Aristotle.

Aristotle as we had said earlier was a pupil of Plato. He stayed in Plato's Academy for twenty years. He distinguished himself as an outstanding student and devoted his time to the study of the great systems that were in vogue. He gathered information about the life of Socrates from Plato and the extant works that were available in the Academy at that time. From his association with Plato, he came to gain first hand insight into the real teachings of Socrates. Being of a prodigious disposition, he was able to discern and analyze a lot of the knotting problems with a view to making them more accessible to men that are not richly imbued with the capacity for intellectual rigor. In his treatise, he deals with Socrates in a brief manner but his main interest lay in trying to clarify the origin of transcendental form. Since most of his writings are based on facts drawn from history, we find them highly secondary. It is this that has made many historians of philosophy to hold that Aristotle offers nothing essential about Socrates which was not already contained in the Platonic dialogues. This means that his views may not be valuable as an independent source. But as one that was known for his mental excellence, he must have through his readings been able to shed light on some dark corners of the writings of his predecessors or at least helped to tighten certain loose ends that might exist in the reconstruction of the philosophy of Socrates. If his views fail to equal those of Plato, Xenophon and Aristophanes, at least, it is still useful as a secondary source.

Coming to the question of reconstruction perse, we find that we have actually looked at the principal sources. Being left in the maze of indecision, we shall now take a close look at the corollary of the views of these different reporters, and then know what the nature that is, the life and teachings of Socrates are all about.

When we look at the foregoing four sources with perspicacity and caution, we will discover that Socrates had been portrayed as in many lights as the sources are. The problem arises because no matter the source one uses in reconstructing Socrates, the fact remains that the description cannot be all embracing and therefore must be lacking in some details and hence inadequate. For example, if one takes Xenophon as our source, one is bound to perceive Socrates as one who was chiefly concerned with making good men and citizens. This we know was not the only concern of Socrates. Again, if we base our source on Plato's dialogues, what will be evinced in us, is a man who was concerned with laying a foundation for transcendentalism. This account again is inadequate because we know that Socrates was more than a metaphysician. If we percolate our information through Aristotle, we are presented with a man who was not the initiator of Platonic theory of forms. In our opinion, to fully understand and reconstruct the philosophy of Socrates, there is need for us to reconstruct his philosophy from a pedestal that will be all encompassing and therefore detailed. All the perspectives must be made use of. It is only in this way that a total, consistent and objective picture of Socrates can be formed. In the Platonic dialogues, we find Socrates being used as the mouthpiece of Plato in the communication of certain ideas. But the problem is that their views appear to be intricately interwoven and any attempt at extrication will continue to be an exercise in futility. But be that as it may, we shall not despair in our task of reconstructing the philosophy of Socrates.

Making useful our foregoing revelations, we shall now attempt a reconstruction of the philosophy of Socrates. Socrates is known to be the true initiator of a new epoch and is also known as one who produced a revolution in philosophy. His critical skill and high philosophical inclination are said to be instrumental to the profundity of issues that characterize the philosophical discourse of his time. From what we have seen so far, it becomes clear that Socrates philosophy must be seen in the light of his contributions in morals, epistemology, metaphysics and politics. This would mean approaching the issue from a broad perspective. This means that the view points of Plato, Xenophon, Aristotle and Aristophanes would be harnessed to achieve this completeness.

In the first place, Socrates must be seen as somebody who had something quite new to offer. He was concerned with the existence of man on earth. He did not believe that the sojourn of man to this earth is fortuitous. If this is so, then greater honour and respect are due to the providential force that is responsible for man's coming to be. It is because of this that Socrates constantly fixed his moral gaze at the inscription at the Delphic oracle which reads "Man know thyself". Many philosophers have actually found it difficult to capture the philosophical underpinnings of this all important dictum. Viewed at its face value, it might look meaningless but a rational insight would reveal that there could be more to this short but semantically condensed sentence. It is our view that the importance of this saying lies in the fact that, man cannot conveniently know himself, if he is not sufficiently aware of why he belongs to a particular genus, a word, which Socrates gave its first important interpretation. Man is imbued with a soul which is the pilot that steers our bodily actions. This is only possible if the body is subordinated to the wise counseling of the soul. But how can man be aware of this transcendental truth if he does not pry deep into himself to unravel the complexities that are intricately joined together in the threshold of the subconscious. Man finds himself in a difficult position, that is, that of having to firmly decide what he wants to do in the face of multifarious alternatives. For a wise choice to be taken, Socrates enjoined that man must look more inward with a view to affording himself better understanding of the "self" in him. Little wonder then, that a lot of historians have presented him as somebody who was more "pro-psychology" than "pro-science". But the truth is that, Socrates believes that truth can be better grasped from within before any external speculation can be worthwhile. To him morals should be subordinated to science only because science ensures the systematicity of our thinking process. But out of all sciences, it appears that he treasures moral science most. To him it is a conscious appraisal of oneself that provides the grounds against skepticism. One is surer with truths ascertained from one's constitution that from things that are external to him. Here, we discover the germ of the Cartesian subjective methodology of "I think therefore I am". In this respect also, Socrates differs from Bacon who was particularly obsessed with the question of establishing mastery over the different physical object that exist around us. Bacon was concerned with the progress of physics and the use of induction in scientific enterprise. However, Socrates applied a different meaning when he used induction. To him, it is a method which entails moving from propositions best known to those of the term. For instance, we are aware of the problems of induction by simple enumeration. It leads to hasty generalization, since it allows that we conclude after a limited number of instances have been observed.

Socrates saw himself as a midwife who being barren, was compensated with the ability of knowing how to help men in "labour of ideas" to put to bed these ideas that have been hiding away in the dark crevices of their minds. To him, men are endowed with ideas they know not about. It is through conversation (dialectics) and definitions that these ideas are elicited. A correct definition is held to be a true description of the thing perse. Aristotle rightly attributed to him the father of abstract definitions and inductive reasoning. This means that he actually started the search for standardized definitions of concepts. This actually was motivated by the fact that Socrates consciously pursued his search for the essence of things believing that true knowledge consists in true definitions.

To Aristophanes, Socrates is just one who like the sophists concerned himself with high speculation about the far removed while the pressing issues are neglected to the peril of men. This view actually is not altogether true. Although Socrates sought for the kind of truth that will break the bounds of ephemerality, he still concerned himself with the self which is part of the transient world. Aristophanes has been presented as one who knew little of Socrates and who merely used Socrates as a comic. But the point is that it will be most improper for a satirist like Aristophanes to use Socrates that openly if Socrates never possessed the qualities that he attributed or ascribed to him. The fact may be that, he might have actually abstracted the qualities in Socrates that were crucial or germane for his artistic message. Socrates was a moralist, who considered virtue to be knowledge. This at least shows that Socrates had other important spheres that he directed his attention to.

To Xenophon Socrates completely denounced physical speculations and occupied himself with how to bring about a moral revolution in the lives of people. This means that Socrates is one who did much to influence the moral standing of his time. This is of course true but it will be myopic to conclude that this is all that Socrates concerned himself about. It is actually in his methods that he made serious marks and will continue to be esteemed in this light. Socrates is an epitome of moral uprightness, but he clearly made contributions in other fields. To Plato, Socrates is the true colossus of philosophic wisdom and the true master of all lovers of wisdom. Plato attributes every of his ideas to his master Socrates, be they in his metaphysics, politics and ethics. Like his master, he believed that only a wise man can be truly courageous, just and temperate. He held that there is a rational insight through which man comes to be acquainted with indubitable truths that are universal and objective. He also holds like his master that man should be upright in all his deeds and should always be prepared to give up his life in times when it is glorifying to do so. He also held that knowledge is innate and as such should be reawakened and tapped for the task of better organization of human life. He also held that the senses are deceptive and should be subordinated to the soul. The point here is that, Plato explicitly as his master did, believed in the immortality of the soul, that is, the fact that the soul survives after death. This is the lesson that Plato learned from Socrates' death, at least, that a philosopher is not supposed to fear death since his soul will be spared the trouble of earthly imperfections, and released for the glory of immutable truths that exist in the bosom of world of forms. The notion of excellence in politics is possibly "a carried forward" attitude of Socrates who in his actions and words believed that only the best was good enough. He believed that man could achieve this by carrying out a thorough self examination. To him, "an unexamined life is not worth living". From what we have said so far, it becomes clear that Socrates was instrumental to the noble and extensive ideas that Plato later communicated. So one can say that Socrates brought the seeds while Plato actually did the planting, the tending and the harvesting of the fruits. To both, we are appreciative of their high intellectual capacity. This then follows that to properly conceive Socrates; one must see him as a moralist, a sophist of a kind, a metaphysician, a scientist, and a politician.

Socrates and Sophism
Socrates is regarded as the father of the golden era of philosophy. He stands out a paragon of all virtues and an encyclopedist of first dimension. He was the master and teacher of Plato. He did not put any of his ideas down in written form. Most of what we know of him is received from Plato his ablest pupil. It is the problem of discrimination between his ideas and those of Plato that we call "Socratic problem".

Socrates is classed among the Sophists but he does not see himself as a sophist. He sees himself as antagonistic to the Sophists. In the records of Burnet and Taylor, Socrates is seen as a Sophist. The following quotation bears this out. Of all the men whom the Athenians of the late fifth century know as "Sophists" or teachers of wisdom, the noted was Socrates. Socrates is said to have a lot in common with the Sophists. For example, they all had the youths as their audience; they were all itinerant teachers, they taught knowledge that kicked against traditional Greek beliefs, they were opposed to certain religious beliefs and the Homeric conception of the gods and their aim was to liberate the youths from the shackles of ignorance.

The difference between Socrates and the Sophists can be found in the following:
(1)   Socrates did not charge fees for his teaching

(2) He did not teach his wisdom nor did he belief that truth was relative. Rather he sought for eternal and objective truths which are fixed.

(3) Socrates was more concerned with building up the moral character of the youth than in preparing the youths for political life. He was not concerned with rhetoric or eristics.

(4) Socrates was opposed to empty claim of the Sophists. He busied himself to dash their cocksureness and destroy their arrogance and pride.

(5) While the Sophists claimed to know all things, Socrates feigned ignorant of any knowledge. The Delphic oracle declared Socrates as the wisest man. According to Socrates, this is because he acknowledged his own ignorance unlike the Sophists who claimed to know while they knew nothing. He makes good the saying that "He who knows not and knows not that he knows not is an incorrigible fool – such was the state of the Sophists.

Background

Socrates was not a mythical person; he was a philosopher who lived in the fifth century BC. His father was Sophroniscus and His mother Phanarete. He got married to Xantippe.

He took part in soldiering and in the political life of Athens of his time. He was a vigorous citizen and a stickler for moral excellence and wisdom.

Socratic Method

Socrates bequeathed to us what is called the midwifery method or the conversational method otherwise called the Dialectical method. His mother Phanaerete was a midwife and Socrates claimed that like his mother, he helps men who are laden with the labour of ideas to be delivered of such ideas safe and sound. He says that men have latent ideas which they are unconscious of. These ideas can be stimulated and brought to the fore through the process of question and answer or the conversational method.

Dialectics is a kind of dialogue where through the art of question and answer the real essence of concepts are captured leaving out the noxious or otherwise accepted but not real definition of concepts. It is a method through which universal definitions of concepts are sought.

His Philosophical Teachings

It is more in the realm of morality that Socrates' teachings are felt. He was regarded as paragon of all virtues. He taught the virtues of humility, courage, sincerity, uprightness, dedication, devotion and loyalty. His preoccupation was how to make good men out of his audience especially the youths. He was concerned with living in conformity with one's teaching.

He is popular for the saying that "the unexamined life is not worth living". We also owe a lot to him for his counsel of "Man know thyself". He was of the view that error comes from ignorance and "knowledge was virtue". To know the right is to do the right. His moral life is well presented in Plato's dialogues like [Crito], [Apology], etc. In these dialogues, we see Socrates willing to pay the price for his life of uprightness though falsely accused; he refused to take the opinion for exile. He preferred to die at the instance of the Athenian courts decision that he should die. He philosophized that death is not evil to a good man and more so to a philosopher because it provides him a passage to go and be with the gods and as a philosopher (a lover of truth) to return to the bosom of truth and knowledge.

In his metaphysics, he is said to be the author of immortality of the soul, the transcendentalism of forms, of the possibility of universal definitions and is the purveyor of the tripartite nature of the soul and that of inductive reasoning.

Socrates is important as the key figure that opened up the door way to moral philosophy. He was the first to show that philosophy has affinity with practical life and he ended up a martyr of his philosophical conviction. He was accused of not worshipping the gods whom the state worships, and for introducing new and unfamiliar religions. He was also accused of corrupting the Athenian youths. Though these accusations were unfounded, he surrendered willfully to the "superior" verdict of the Athenian judges.

CHAPTER TWELVE

THE GOLDEN ERA OF GREEK PHILOSOPHY II

Plato 348-347 BC
Background
It is in Plato that we witness the completeness of Greek thought and the flowering of Greek genius. Plato is the first Greek philosopher to attempt a comprehensive view in matters of knowledge. He is said to have been born in the year 428/27BC which was the year of Pericles death. His father was Ariston and his mother Perictone. His was of a distinguished Athenian family. His family belonged to the elite of the Periclean age and was influential in the Athenian public life. Plato in a similar vein was being prepared for a future political role, but fate changed this family aspiration. The very cruel way in which his master Socrates was killed during the period of the restored Athenian democracy discouraged him from continuing with the vision of pursuing a political career.

Early Influences
Plato no doubt was influenced by the views of all the philosophers before him. He was however particularly influenced by the views of Cratylus a disciple of Heraclitus, Parmenides, the Pythagoreans, and majorly by Socrates who was his mentor and benefactor. From these influences he learnt the fact of change among physical things, the permanence of Being, the importance of mathematics and the possibility of a transcendental conception of reality. He founded a school called the Academy the equivalent of a University in the then known world.

His Works
Plato was highly prolific, he wrote many books and in dialogue form. Dialogues are in the form of lively conversation, with an exchange of ideas that progressively penetrate and clarify the subject or concept at issue. Some of these dialogues include the Republic (which is apparently the most widely read of the

dialogues), others are Apology, Charmides, Crito, Euthyphro, Lysis, Protagoras, Ion, Laches, Gorgias, Meno, Euthydemus, Hippias, Cratylus, Menexenus, Theaetetus, Parmenides, Sophist, Politicus, Philebus, Timaecus, Critias, Epinomis, etc. These dialogues deal on different themes with contents that focus on Epistemology, Metaphysics, Morality, Politics, aesthetics, Mathematics, Geometry, etc.

His Philosophical Teachings

It is almost platitudinous to say that philosophy is nothing but a series of footnotes to Plato and Aristotle. Their works were wide-ranging touching on many areas of knowledge, teaching very worthy lessons to the philosophical world. We shall examine briefly Plato's contribution to the body of knowledge in the different (major) areas of philosophy.

Epistemology or Theory of Knowledge

Epistemology is coined from two Greek words "episteme which means knowledge and "logos" which means to study or reason out. Epistemology can therefore mean systematic study about knowledge.

The Skeptics and the sophists had denied the possibility of certain or objective knowledge. For Gorgias, knowledge was impossible and incommunicable. For Heraclitus, all things are in a state of flux and as such nothing can be grasped since things change, they cannot be known because before we know them they have changed. For Parmenides, there is nothing that changes. What is, is and cannot change. Being is stable, fixed and unchanging. This means that reality is different from appearance. For Parmenides the way of truth is the way of fixed reality. A thing cannot be itself and another thing (its opposite) at the same time.

When Plato came, he tried to harmonize the views of Heraclitus and Parmenides. Plato averred that physical things are fleeting and changeable. This means that unchanging fixed, permanent reality can only be found in another world realm. Plato posited that there exists another world where real things exist. This he calls the world of ideas. For Plato, knowledge is possible through a rigorous training of the mind to behold "the form of the good" which illuminates reality. These facts are illustrated by Plato through what he calls allegories of the cave, the divided line and world of forms.

For Plato, we do not learn anything what we do is to recollect what we had known before. This is what he calls his theory of Recollection or Reminiscence. He illustrated this through the slave boy who though had never learned Geometry, was able through question and answer to show that he has some knowledge of geometry which he never learned. This can be found in his dialogue [Meno].

His Metaphysics

Metaphysics means the science of being or existence. It deals with what there is, the nature of reality and the relationship among things. For Plato, there are two types of existence, physical and transcendental. Physical existence is ephemeral and changing while transcendental existence is fixed, permanent and reliable. He calls this reliable reality "forms". This led him to postulate the theory of immortality of the soul and the theory of pre-existence. He said that the soul of man had existed in the world of ideas before being born into the physical realm. All learning took place in the previous world; all that happens now is that we are reminded of what we had known before.

The physical objects are mere copies of their originals (prototype or archetype) in the world of forms. He says that through participation and approximation, exemplification and approximation physical things gain their nature from the world of forms. This means that physical things participate in the real things in the world of forms, they approximate the nature of the real and try to appropriate and exemplify and instantiate these essences in the world of forms. This means that in the world of forms, we have ideal man, table, chair, dog, lion, etc., of which the physical counterparts are mere exemplifications or poor copies. These ideal prototypes are called universals.

His Moral Philosophy
His epistemology runs through his metaphysics, ethics and politics. Plato disagreed with the Sophists that moral rules are unnatural, relative and fleeting. Plato presented a strong argument to show that moral rules are universal, stable and fixed. For example, justice cannot be one thing now and another thing later. Or, one thing in one culture and another thing in another culture. It should be the same thing constituting of the same essence. Killing cannot be good in one culture and bad in another.

He discountenanced the view of the Sophists (Thrasymachus) that "might was right" and that "justice is the interest of the stronger". Rather justice is attending to the interest of the weaker party. Justice is the harmonious working of the component parts of the soul, so that none usurps or suppresses the other. Like Socrates, Plato admits that knowledge is virtue and that error or wrong doing is as a result of ignorance. To achieve harmony, the rational part of the soul should keep the spirited and the appetitive parts of the soul under check. The soul is divided into three: (1) the rational (2) the spirited (3) the appetitive parts. Proper existence will entail harmony, good behaviour and the following of reasoned moral pathways rather than arbitrary public opinion. Our conduct should be in line with what is eternally good and not with the relative standards of good based on faulty human perception.

His Political Theory
In his political theory, Plato was propelled by the evil he saw in the restored democracy of the fifth century to philosophize deeply on the concept of politics. The most penetrating theory of politics in the ancient period came from Plato. He saw the problem in politics as resulting from having the wrong people at the helm of political affairs.

To solve the problem of degeneracy in politics, he enunciated a conception of the state which outlines how the state should be conceived and administered. He started by working at the construction of the individual, he identified three parts of the soul; that is the rational, the spirited and the appetitive. He stated that justice can be achieved in the individual through the harmonious functioning of the above three parts. He saw a correlation between the individual and the state. He said that the state is "the individual writ large". He identified three component parts of the state namely (1) the guardian class or the philosopher kings, (2) the auxiliary class or the soldiers and (3) the artisan class or the menial workers. He posited that there will be harmony in the state if these three classes are identified, given appropriate training and made to perform their legitimate and appropriate functions without each usurping the function of the other, there will be peace and justice in the body politic.

The most important of the classes is the guardian class. He emphasized the need to be given rigorous training like training in music (harmonics), geometry, mathematics, censored literature, military training, dialectics and other requisite leadership training. This is to ensure that he grasps the "vision of the Good" which will enable him to distinguish good from bad and to pursue the course of justice in administration. This trained ruler(s) he calls philosopher king(s). He had a lot of prescriptions for them. He talked of communism of wives, communism of property, communism of children through Eugenic breeding (reproduction based on the mating of the best human beings—male an female with the view of reproducing geniuses). The idea is to deliver the rulers from the obsession of private property or private family. This arrangement is envisaged will enhance their efficiency and loyalty.

Plato said that the nations of men will never cease from trouble until either the true and genuine breed of philosophers shall come to politics or until the rulers in the Polis shall come by some divine ordinance take to the true pursuit of philosophy. It is true philosophy alone that can lead to a true discernment of justice, public and private.

The ideal state is patterned after aristocracy. Aristocracy may degenerate into timocracy (love or honour) then, to plutocracy (concern here is wealth) then to democracy (a chaotic system where all pursue their own freedom and equality) and finally to despotism.

(This is where one man dominates the whole state caring for his own interests).

We conclude again with the following words "until philosophers are kings; or the kings and princes of this world have the spirit and power of philosophy and political greatness and wisdom meet in one, cities, nations will never have rest from their evils".

In the Laws Plato developed the second best state. This state must be established on clean slate with a completely new generation that will be brought up in good laws from infancy and who would adhere to the laws voluntarily. Plato's aim in his political theory was to achieve a political state where justice is entrenched, where there is harmony; and where the rulers are wise, the soldiers are courageous and the masses are temperate. The philosopher king has the vision of wisdom and he rules not with laws but through ingrained wisdom. A system of government that operates with laws is the second best state. In the Republic Plato talks about the ideal state. The major critique of Plato's political theory is that it is utopian and idealistic.

CHAPTER THIRTEEN

THE GOLDEN ERA OF GREEK PHILOSOPHY III

Aristotle
Background
Aristotle was born in 384 BC in Stagira in Thrace. His father Nicomachus was the physician to the king of Macedon, Amytas the second. Aristotle came to Athens in 367BC and joined Plato's Academy at the age of seventeen. He stayed at the Academy for twenty years. After the death of Plato, the Academy came under the control of Speucippus Plato's nephew.

In 335 Aristotle set up his own institution called Lyceum at the North East end of Athens. He was here for about twelve years. He is said to have taken up the tutorship of Alexander the Great who succeeded his father. After the death of Alexander the Great, there arose a wave of Macedonian feeling. Aristotle escaped saying he will not allow the Athenians to commit the second crime against philosophy, the murder of Socrates being the first.

Influences
Aristotle like Plato was influenced by all the philosophers that came before him including Socrates and Plato. In Plato's Academy, he studied wide ranging subjects and thoughts of other philosophers. However, as his views matured, he became more and more independent in thought. He was greatly influenced by Plato whose terminologies he borrowed and used. The difference between Plato and Aristotle lay more in their different temperaments and ideologies. Plato was concerned with ideal and transcendental knowledge while Aristotle was concerned with the physical and the realistic. This can be gleaned from their research interests, while Plato was interested in mathematics with its attendant universal forms which tended to point to reality beyond the senses; Aristotle was interested in biology and other natural sciences where objects were subject to sense perception. This made Aristotle to see reality in physical things.

Aristotle's Writings

Aristotle was a copious writer, writing in treatise form and on extensive subject matters. Cicero described him as "an eloquent, charming and polished writer who pours out a golden stream of eloquence". While many of his works are extant, others are said to have been lost. He is regarded as the first philosopher that wrote like a professor. Some of his works were classed as esoteric and highly technical. In the traditional *Corpus Aristotelicum*, the treatise are grouped in an order that is based on their subject matter, we have those logic like (1) the categories (2) De interpretatione (3) Topics (4) Prior and posterior Analytics (5) Sophistical Refutations. On physics we have eight books like (1) Decaelo (2) De Generatione ET corruptione (3) Meteorologica (4) De Anima (5) Parva Naturalia, etc. On Natural History we have (1) History of Animals (2) Parts of Animals (3) Generation of Animals (4) Movement of Animals (5) Progression of Animals. We also have his metaphysics (a name to his book which came after those on physical nature by Andronicus of Rhodes who chronicled Aristotle's works). We also have his Nichomachean and Eudemian Ethics. We have his politics. Some of his other works are in dialogue form (they are nineteen in number) example are Manexenus, symposium, sophist and statesman which are names also for Plato's dialogue. He wrote on justice, On Rhetoric, On the Soul, etc, (others are on kingship, on the Good, on ideas, on Democritus, on the Pythagoreans, on contraries) (OWENS 1959, 285-292).

His Philosophical Teachings

LOGIC: It was Aristotle who invented formal logic. He also invented the idea of separate sciences. He saw logic as a vertical instrument with which to formulate language properly when analyzing what a science involves. Aristotlelian logic is the study of the thought for which words are signs. It is an attempt to get at truth by an analysis of the thought that reflects our understanding of things (STUMPF 1971, 88). To carry out any reasoning about things which must understand the nature of substance? Substance has subject and predicates. These predicates feature as the categories (1) quality (2) quantity (3) relation (4) place (5) date (6) posture (7) possession (8) action (9) passivity. Predicates are accidents which are used to describe a thing or substance.

It was Aristotle that gave us the form of logic called syllogism. Syllogism is a discourse in which certain things being stated, a necessary conclusion follows from the propositions being stated. For example, if we say that
All men are mortal
Socrates is a man
Therefore, Socrates is mortal; the conclusion follows from the first two premises.

HIS METAPHYSICS: Metaphysics is the title given to Aristotle's works which came after those titled physics. The term metaphysics simply means after physics. Others have taken metaphysics to mean any discourse that is beyond those of physical nature. Metaphysics is the science of being, existence, relation and essence. In metaphysics we consider issues like appearance and reality, notion of being, essence, causality, universal, body-mind problem, substance, freedom and determinism, etc.

In his metaphysics, Aristotle talked about matter and form. Every object has two aspects, the unchanging aspect "matter" and the changing aspect "form". He talked about four principal causes namely (1) material (2) formal (3) efficient and (4) final cause. That is, the material out of which a thing is made, the shape it takes, the maker and the purpose for which the object is made respectively.

Aristotle talked about potentiality and actuality. Only God is full actuality, every other thing is potentiality that is, in a state of becoming. He said that every motion is initiated by another but this series of motions can only terminate in a first mover which he calls the unmoved mover. God is this unmoved mover.

HIS ETHICS: Aristotle is famous for his doctrine of the golden mean. He says that a good action is one which aims at the mean between excess and defect. Example courage is the mean between fool hardiness (excess) and cowardice (defect). Aristotle adopted a teleological approach to ethics. Every action is aimed at the achievement of some particular good. The highest good which he calls the "Somum bonum" is happiness. Happiness is the chief end of all actions. This is achieved through contemplation. His theory of ethics is based on moderation. However, his list of virtues at some points run contrary to those of Christian ethics. For example, he endorses pride as a virtue and humility as a vice. He argues that a free born citizen should be proud of his birth. Humility is a defect as it is humiliating and debasing.

He identified three types of friendship, namely; friendship based on utility (1) what we can gain from each other (2) Friendship based on pleasure-(sensual pleasure) and (3) friendship based on goodness (this is the best type of friendship). It is not based on ulterior motives but on goodness itself.

HIS POLITICAL PHILOSOPHY: For Aristotle, the state comes into being because of the need for the good life and self sufficiency. Thy individual, the family, the small community discovered that they cannot take care of all their needs. This gave rise to coming together of many communities to form a state so that the needs of the citizens can be met through the pulling of their resources together. The formation of the state is therefore, the necessary entailment of man's desire to attain self-sufficiency.

Every man has the need to be in a society. He says that "he who is unable to live in society or who has no need because he is sufficient for himself, must be either a beast or a god". The formation of the state like the family is a natural process.

Aristotle endorses the necessity for slaves. He says that some people are naturally created to serve as slaves. For him; there are certain menial jobs which will be unsuitable for freeborn to do, so the slaves are by nature suited for such jobs.

Aristotle was very critical of Plato's theory of communism of wives, property and children. He sees it as a violation of man's natural right to own property. He says that men do better when set at work on that which is there own. It is a truism that "that which is common to the greatest number has the least care bestowed upon it". Communism of children will mean that the children will be denied the necessary filial affection.

Aristotle identified certain forms of governments (constitutions) and their pervasions. We have kingship (monarchy), aristocracy, and polity with their corresponding pervasions as tyranny, oligarchy and democracy. For him the best form of government is polity of constitutional government. This type of government is defined as that state in which the citizens at large administer the state for the common interest. Aristotle sees democracy as the worst form of government because here, the unguarded mob exercise rule and this ends up in chaos and disorder.

With the above we conclude by saying that ancient period of philosophy is marked by a systematic and progressive development, with their perfect culmination in the philosophies of Plato and Aristotle.

Fundamental Issues in Aristotle's Philosophy
Background to Aristotle's Basic Works in Philosophy
Here we shall treat in detailed form Aristotle's main contributions to philosophy already discussed in summary above. Aristotle wrote a vast number of works but only a few of them survived till date. Following the lead of his teacher (Plato), Aristotle apparently composed dialogues intended for a general audience, many of them on political subjects; except for few fragmentary citations, nothing remains of these. The surviving works are principally Treatises, which are thought to have been prepared in connection with his different researches and teachings. Although, deeply influenced by Plato, Aristotle seem never to have been an orthodox Platonist. Evidently, he developed many of his characteristic doctrines while he was still in the academy and he contended for the leadership of Plato's followers at the time of Plato's death but lost out to Speusppius . According to Thomas Mautner, who commented on Aristotle's works, in the [Penguin Dictionary of Philosophy] states:

Aristotle published dialogues and other popular writings from an early period, but the publication of his lecture years after his death eventually caused the dialogues to be neglected: they are known to us now only from fragments and reports. The extensive treatise that have come down to us represent, many, but not all of his lectures. (MAUTNER 1996, 40)

He tried as a very serious scholar to put down things on paper. The range of his interest is indicated by a list of some of his important writings, such as: *Categories* (kinds of predications or basic classifications of existing things; *Prior Analytics* (The first treatise ever written on logic); *Posterior Analytics* (philosophy of science and theory of knowledge); *Physics* (Principles of science); *De anima* (psychology); *Metaphysics* (Analysis of being qua being); *Nicomachean Ethics* (Moral Theory); *Politics* (Political Theory); Poetic (Literary Writings). In addition, he wrote extensively on biology and on such diverse topics as dialectics, rhetorics,chemistry, geology, meterology and cosmology. One can say, without mincing words that Aristotle almost covered all areas or subjects of human endeavor. Aristotle's vastness in knowledge, made him not be a thorough going academic, as it pertains to having an area of specialization both in philosophy and the biological or natural and applied sciences per se. Will Durant has this to say about him:

> Naturally, in a mind of such scientific turn, poesy was lacking. We must not expect of Aristotle such literary brilliance as floods the pages of dramatist—philosopher, Plato, instead of giving us great literature , in which philosophy is embodied in myth and imagery, Aristotle gives us science, technical, abstract, concentrated…gifts. Instead of giving terms to literature as Plato did he built the terminology of sciences and philosophy. We can hardly speak of any term today in sciences without employing terms which he invented, they lie like fossil in the strata of our speech. (1995, 50)

It is possible that the writings attributed to Aristotle may not be his, but then, those of his students and compilation of his followers who have embalmed the unadorned substance of his lectures in their notes. It does not appear as if Aristotle published any known work in his life time, except those on logic and rhetorics. In the case of his metaphysics and politics, it is believed that his student, especially Andronicus of Rhodes packaged and edited them.

Aristotle's Metaphysics
The central issues in Aristotle's metaphysics revolve around the study of being as being. The fundamental question asked in this regard is that; "what is being?" What constitutes the beingness of being? In other words, what constitutes the thingness of things? What makes our world a world of things at all? The integrity of the world as a world and of anything in it which endures as itself for any time at all, is not self-explanatory. It is something to be wondered at and pondered about its causes.

We are taught that a moving thing, if nothing disturbs it, will continue moving forever. It is certainly true that a heavy thing in motion is as hard to stop as it was to set in motion, and that we cannot set out of moving automobiles without continuing, for a while, to share their motions. But these are evidences of persistent motion, not at all the same thing as inertia of motion. There is no evidence of the latter. In principle, there cannot be, because we cannot abolish all the world to observe an undisturbed moving thing. There is a powerful and in itself own way, beautiful account of the world, which assumes inertia, appealing to those experiences which suggest that motion at an unchanging speed is a state no different from the rest. The hidden premise which leads from that step to the notion of inertia is the assumption that rest is an inert state; if it is not, the same evidence could lead to the conclusion that an unchanging speed is fragile and vulnerable, as unlikely and as hard to come by as an unchanging thing. We may then raise the questions: How can a balloon remain unchanged? It does so only so long as the air inside pushes out no harder and no less hard than the air outside pushed in; is the air inside the balloon at rest? Can it be at rest as long as it is performing a task? Can the balloon be at rest if there is air inside? The answer is quite clear and simple; it cannot be. It can certainly remain in a place like other apparently inert things, such as table. If you pull a leg from under a table the top would fall. Leave together and leave alone, they will remain without moving to anywhere. The question would then be, is the table at rest?. These puzzle questions will find meaningful expressions in Aristotle's metaphysics of being and essence.

Aristotle is trying to let us know that the least thoughtful, least alert way of being in the world is to regard everything which remains itself as doing so causelessly, inertly. To seek as cause for the being-as-it-is of anything is already to be in the grip of the question Aristotle says must always be asked. To seek the causes and sources of the being-as-it-is of everything that is, is to join Aristotle in which regard every manifestation of persistence, order, or recurrence as a marvel, an achievement. That everything in the world disclosed to our senses is in a ceaseless state of change. He believed that the world hangs together enough to be experienced at all is a fact so large that we rarely take notice of. But the two together change, and a context of persistence out of which can emerge and force one to acknowledge some non–human cause at work: for whichever side of the world–change or rest, order or dissolution-is simply its uncaused, inert way, the other side must be the result of effort. Something must be at work in the world, hidden to us, visible only in its effect, pervading all that is, and it must be either a destroyer or a preserver.

      For his metaphysics Aristotle developed what he called "science of the first philosophy". Throughout his metaphysics, he was so concerned with a type of knowledge that he thought could be most rightly called wisdom. In the inaugural part of his work in metaphysics, he began it with a powerful phrase: "All men desire to know". This innate desire says Aristotle, is only a desire to know in order to do or make something, but a desire of knowing the essence of things. He went on to talk of different forms of knowledge. For Aristotle, some men know only what they experience through the senses, but for him, we do not regard what we know through the senses as wisdom. We do not deny the fact that our most authoritative knowledge of particular things is acquired through our senses, for this kind of knowledge tell us only "the that"of things and not the "why" of things. It tells us for example that fire is not hot, but not "why" it is not hot. Similarly, in medicine some men know that medicine heal certain illnesses. This knowledge based on certain experience is, according to Aristotle , of a lower level than the knowledge of the medical scientist who knows , not only,"that" a medicine will heal, but knows also the reason "why" a particular medicine heals and not the other.

He applauded wisdom so much because, metaphysics pursues wisdom par excellence. That is, wisdom in itself, which deals with the first principles or causes of things, and so it is considered as the universal knowledge of things in their highest degree. This means that it is the science which is removed from immediate senses; it is the most abstract science that deals with the nature of things in their essences. Aristotle, although believes that metaphysics is the most abstract of all sciences, he says it is equally the most exact of all other sciences.

Metaphysics deals with knowledge at the highest level of abstraction. This knowledge is abstract because it is about what is universal as contrasted to that which is particular. Every science has its own level of abstraction in as much as it deals with the first principles or causes of its subject matter. Wisdom has to deal then with the abstract level of knowledge and not with the level of visible things, for Aristotle says, "sense perception is common to all, and therefore easy and no mark of wisdom"— true wisdom. First philosophy or metaphysics is the most abstract and also the most exact of all the sciences because it tries to discover truly the first principle from which even the first principles of the various sciences are derived from. True knowledge is found in what is most knowable and that which is most knowable are the first principles or causes.

Aristotle's metaphysics will be incomplete without making reference to his stand on "substance". For him, substance is

a primary kind of being (or existent or what exists, or what it is). It is what primarily exists. He gives two characteristics of what traditionally we call "substance" as "primacy" and "particularity". Entities in the various category depend on substance for their existence. For Aristotle, as cited by Mautner:
The ultimate realities (primary substances) are concrete things, Aristotle's preferred examples are biological individuals such as Socrates and of concrete things the ultimate realities because if they did not exist nothing else would exist ether. In other words if there were no such things as Socrates', characteristics such as manhood or paleness would have nothing to belong to, and hence they would not exist. (MAUTNER 1996, 41)

Aristotle also recognizes 'secondary' substances such as man, which is the class or the defining property of Socrates, and features such a paleness. It must be borne in mind that John Locke, a progenitor of modern essentialism and a member of the 17th century current of thought in the history of epistemology, made some emphasis on the distinction between primary and secondary qualities of things. A similar distinction is to be found in one of the following philosophers, Democritus and Plato. Aristotle distinguishes those properties of things, which are perceptible by one senses and are therefore common to those senses. In metaphysics, Aristotle stipulates distinctively matter and form, essence and existence, potency and actuality, among others.

Matter and form

On the nature of reality, Aristotle believes that every material thing must compose of matter and form. The matter itself is indeterminate and is determined by the form; for matter is determined by the form it takes, that is, the form of that which determines it. In order words, if matter receives the form of a chair, it becomes a chair. If it receives the form of a flower it becomes a flower. If it receives the form of anything at all, it becomes that particular thing, etc. In this sense, matter is completely indeterminate; it is simply the possibility to receive the form and become the object whose form it receives.

Aristotle maintains that everything that exist is a concrete individual thing, and that everything is a unity of matter and form. Substance, therefore, is a composite of matter and form. It was Plato who earlier argued that ideas or forms, such as manness or tableness, has a separate existence from that particular man or table. Similarly, he treated space as the material substratum or the stuff out of which individual things were made. For Plato, the primary stuff of space was molded by the externally existing form into individual shapes. This was Plato's way of explaining how they could be many individual things that all have one and the same, that is universal nature or essence while being individuals. This universal, Plato said is the form, which exists externally and is separated from any particular thing and is found in each thing only because the thing (table) participates in the form (tableness).

Aristotle rejected Plato's explanation of the universal forms, rejecting specifically the notion that the forms existed separately from individual things. Of course, Aristotle did agree that there are universals, that universals such as man and table are more than merely subjective notions. Indeed, he recognized that without the theory of universal, there could be no scientific knowledge, for then there would be no way of saying something about all members of a particular class. What makes scientific knowledge effective is that it discovers classes of objects (e.g. a certain form of human disease) so that whenever an individual falls into this class, other facts can be assumed to be relevant.

Aristotle was not convinced that Plato's theory of form could help us in acquiring any knowledge at all. In fact, the theory of form, according Aristotle, has compounded the problem it set out to solve. In trying to get at knowledge, you end up multiplying the *explicandum* (that which is to be explained).

Although, Aristotle passes an adverse criticism on the platonic theory of separate Ideas or Forms, he is in full agreement with Plato that the universal is not merely subjective concept or mode of oral expression, for to the universal in the mind there corresponds the specific essence in the object, though this essence does not exist in any state separation 'extra-mentum'; it is separated only in the mind and through the mind's activities. Aristotle was convinced as Plato was, that the universal was the object of science. It follows then that if the universal is in no way real, if it has no objective reality whatsoever, there is no objective scientific knowledge, for science does not deal with individuals as such. The universal is real, it has reality not only in the mind but also in the things, though the existence in the things does not entail that formal universality that it has in the mind. Individual belonging to the same species are real substances, but they do not partake in an objective universal that is numerically the same in all manners of the class. Accordingly, Aristotle as cited by Copleston has this to say:

> The specific essence is numerically different in each individual of the class, but, on the other hand, it is specifically the same in (i.e. they are all alike in species), and this objective similarity is the real foundation for the abstract universal, which has numerical identity in the mind and can be predicated of all the members of the class indifferently. (1967, 301)

Plato and Aristotle agree on the character of true science, namely, that it is directed to the universal elements in things, i.e. .to the specific similarity. The scientist is not concerned with individual bits of gold as individual, but with the essence of gold, with that specific similarity which is found in all the individual bits of gold i.e. supposing that a gold is a specie

Four Causes
In our world, we see a lot of things changing day by day. The word "change" means a lot of things for different people. For Aristotle change means so many things, including motion, growth, decay, generation and corruption. Some of these changes are natural while others are artificial or even products of human arts. Things are always taking on new forms, new life is born and statues are made. Because change always involves taking on new forms; several

questions can be asked concerning the process of change. There is always the 'why' questions.

Aristotle recognizes four causes which he regarded as different answers to "why" questions i.e. different kind of explanations: why is there a statue here? Because it was made by Mike, (efficient or moving cause) with the shape of Athena (formal cause), out of bronze (material Cause), to adorn the temple (final cause). In nature and in arts, the most important cause is the material cause. In natural objects, example animals, the parts exist for the sake of the whole. Indeed, the whole universe is ordered as a whole of parts which function harmoniously together, at large but finite sphere with a spherical Earth at the Centre.

Aristotle's four causes represent a broad pattern or framework for the explanation of anything or everything. (1) The causes are the formal cause which determines what a thing is. (2) the material cause or that out which something or a thing is made. (3). The efficient cause, by what a thing is made, (4) and the final cause, the end, purpose for which it is made.

Aristotle looked at life through the eyes of a biologist. For him nature is life. All things are in motion, in the process of becoming and decaying away. The process of reproduction was for him a clear example of the power inherent in all living things to initiate change, and to reproduce their kind. Summarizing his causes Aristotle said that "all things come into be by some agency and from something. From this biological viewpoint Aristotle was able to elaborate his notion that form and matter never exist separately. In nature generation of new life involves, according to him, first of all, an individual who already possesses the specific form which the offspring will have. (The male parent) must be the matter capable of being the vehicle of the form. (This matter being contributed by the female parent) from this comes a new individual with the same specific form. From this example Aristotle tries to show that change does not involve bringing together formless matter with matter-less form. On the contrary change occurs always in and to something that is already a combination of form and matter and that is on its way to becoming something new or different.

Aristotle's Syllogistic Logic

One of the basic teachings of Aristotle was on his logic popularly called "formal logic". The logic of Aristotle is an analysis of forms of thought. This is an apt characterization; but it would be a very great mistake to suppose that for Aristotle logic concerns the forms of human thinking in such an exclusive way that has no connection with an external reality. He is chiefly concerned with the form of proofs, and he assumes that the conclusion of scientific proofs gives certain knowledge concerning reality. For example, in the syllogism "all men are mortal. Socrates is a man, therefore, Socrates is mortal." It is not merely that the conclusion is deduced correctly from according to the formal laws of logic: Aristotle assumes that the conclusion is verified in reality. He presupposes therefore a realist theory of knowledge and for him, though an analysis of the form of thought is an analysis of the thought that thinks reality, that reproduces it conceptually within itself, and, in the true judgment, makes statements about reality which are verified in the external world. It is an analysis of human thought in its thought about reality, though Aristotle certainly admits that things do not always exist as extra-mental realites precisely as they are conceived by the mind, e.g. the universal. His doctrine of categories clearly illustrates the point, we are making here about Aristotle. As observed by Copletson:

From the logical viewpoint, the categories comprise about the way in which we think about things—for instance, predicating qualities of substance-but at the same times there are ways in which things actually exist: things are substance and actually have accident. The categories demand therefore, not only a logical but also a metaphysical treatment. (1967, 279)

From the above, it is clear that Aristotle's logic must not be likened to the transcendental logic of Kant. This is because it is not concerned to isolate "a priori" form of thought which are contributed by the mind alone in its active process of knowledge.

Aristotle does not raise "the critical problem" he rather assumes realist epistemology in his logic, this means that the categories of thought, which we express in language, are also the objective categories of the external reality.

We have to note that Aristotle did not limit his interest in logic to the relations of propositions to each other or simply to the consistence of language. His chief interest was with the form of proof, and for this reason, he was particularly concerned with what we can state in precise language about reality, about what things exist and why they are as they are. Science as Aristotle understood it consisted of true statements that accounted for the reason why things behave the way they do, and why they have to be as they are. In this case science consist in the knowledge of the fact that and the reason why. It includes both observation and the theory that explains what is observed. For example, one can observe steam coming from a kettle on the stove, but this mere observation does not on its own enable us to define "steam" in any systematic or scientific manner. This is because a scientific statement about this observation would reflect a careful sorting out of the essential elements of this observation. Setting aside all irrelevant details or "accidents" such as the particular fuel used for the fire and the kind vessel used for the water, focusing squarely upon the special kind of events that is, the production of steam, and giving reason for the occurrence of this event by relating heat, water and steam , in such a way that one can know, have proof , why under such condition heat and water produce steam. The most important thing about science is the language in which it is formulated in logic. Scientific language must indicate as precisely as possible what constitute the distinctive subject matter of a science and it must describe why things act the way they do. From our reflection so far, we can say that logic is the study of words and language, not the way a grammarian would study it. Aristotle is known as the father of "logic" and for him. Logic is the study of thought which words are signs. It is an attempt to get at truth by analysis of the thought that reflects our apprehension or understanding of the nature of things.

In a nutshell, for Aristotle, logic is an instrument of analysis of human thought as it thinks about reality. An important area of Aristotelian logic is his treatment of syllogism. He looks at syllogism as a discourse in which certain things being stated, something other than what is stated follows of necessity from their being so. This is the principle of implication, and Aristotle was particularly concerned that scientific discourse should proceed from one valid step to another with precision. He wanted to discover the rules that would guarantee that conclusion were rightly inferred from their premises. How, then, could one be sure that a conclusion follows from its premises? Or what makes it possible for us, assuming that we have two propositions, to derive from these a third proposition? Aristotle thought that he has discovered the answer to these questions in the basic structure of the syllogism. What exactly is this syllogism? The syllogism is a special form of connected language, 'scientific demonstrations are possible because certain words stand for certain properties, qualities, or characteristics of things. Such words stand for essential properties as compared with accidental properties. To say that a man is mortal is to describe one of his essential properties but to say that he has a brown hair is to talk about his accidental properties.

It has to be pointed out immediately that although Aristotle's doctrine of syllogism is a tool for determining which relationships between premises and conclusion are consistent; his chief interest in developing the syllogism was not simply to assure consistent reasoning. His aim was to provide an instrument for scientific demonstration, and for this reason, he emphasized the relationship between logic and metaphysics, between our way of knowing and what things are and how they behave. That is, he thought that words and things are linked together because the things which language mirrors are also linked together. He equally recognized that it is possible to employ the syllogism consistently without necessarily arriving at science or truth if the premises did not rest upon valid assumptions. He distinguished three kinds of reasoning, each using syllogism. There is dialectical reasoning which is reasoning from opinions that are generally accepted. Second, there is eristic or contentious reasoning, which begins with opinion that seem to be generally accepted but are really not; and the third, there is what he calls demonstrative reasoning, where the premises from which reasoning starts are true and primary. The value of syllogistic reasoning depends very much on the accuracy of the premises. If scientific knowledge is to be achieved, it is necessary that the statement one employs be more than opinion or even probable truth.

Aristotle's Political Theory
Aristotle's political theory is not far-fetched from his notion of morality. Thus, for him, the effectiveness of any political setting must be blended with morality. In collected works; [The Politics] and [Nichomachean Ethics], Aristotle discussed clearly the issues of the natural origin of the state, nature of the human person, common good, justice, forms of government, sovereign (authority) and subordinate relationship, slave and master relationship and the structure of political community in general.

In his political theory, Aristotle has a unique conception of the state and the human person. The creation of state for Aristotle and his master Plato has a natural cause of existence. While the later philosophers like Thomas Hobbes and Jacque Rousseau see the creation of the state from the point of social contract whereby the individuals submit their freedom and will for effective governance. Unlike Plato who sees the economic ends as a strong factor that motivates the existence of a state, Aristotle goes beyond this to see that the function of the state is to ensure the supreme good of humanity. It is an instrument whereby she organizes her members, distributes resources and ensures the common good of all. For Aristotle, justice and fairness have to be promoted in a state for the advantage of the citizens. And a citizen is one who shares in governing and is being governed [The Politics, Bk 111, ah. 13, $1283^b 40$]. In this regard, politics as conceived by Aristotle becomes an act of governance. The main aim of politics is to ensure a free and fair society, goal-orientedness and the well-being of all members in a given political community (State).

Aristotle, in his writing, is of the opinion that politics is an inherent principle in man and it is only possible in an organized group such as the state where people can interact, share resources for the benefit of all. And it is only man that is endowed with the special gift of creativity and intelligence. This is evidence in man's ability to organize his environment, manage his resources and direct the affairs of all the members.

In his conception of human nature, Aristotle recognizes that the human person is endowed with special gifts, which make him different from lower animals. Man for Aristotle is a rational, political as well as moral being. He is capable of developing intellectual and moral virtues by his nature.

Aristotle's conception of the human nature is peculiar in the sense that this conception also motivates him to see man as distinct from the lower animals. In his famous work called *The Soul* (De Anima), Aristotle underscored the constitutive elements of human nature. The soul (psyche) Aristotle refers to it as "life". Aristotle observed that in nature, there are vegetative life, animal life and rational life. Among these forms of life, Aristotle notes that "man is the only living thing that manifest rationality to any marked degree".

On human nature, Aristotle further realizes that man is a composite being. In his dual nature, man is made up of body and soul. The soul, for Aristotle, is the rational part of man while the body is the passionate or the emotional part of man. In the latter part, man shares with the lower animals. But in the former part, man makes himself distinct from the rest of the animals. Aristotle believes that the soul being rational part of man enables him to exercise his intelligence, creativity and freedom. In his view, Aristotle states that "the soul rules over the body with a despotically rule" [The Politics, Bk. 1, ch. 5, 1254^b4]. Aristotle goes further to affirm that the rule of the soul over the body... Is natural and expedient; whereas the equality of the two or the rule of the inferior is always heart-full [The politics, Bk1, ch. 5, 1254^b5].

Aristotle sees the soul as intellect and the body as appetite or passion.

From the dual nature of man, Aristotle observes that intellective aspect of man (reside in the soul), makes man distinct it is also called rational part of man. But in emotive part (body) man shares certain irrational elements with the lower animals. As Hambrecht states, Aristotle's conception of human nature can be explained in 3 forms. (1) The irrational part which is not subject to rational control. (2) The irrational part which is subject to rational control. (3) And the rational part. Corresponding to the irrational part of human nature ethic is not subject to control by reason is natural excellence (LAMBRECHT 1995, 62). Here, Aristotle observes that there are certain features which the human person possesses that characterized his physical condition. E.g. one is born ugly. The other handsome; one born a slave, the other a master etc. Corresponding to the irrational part of human nature which is subject to being controlled by reason, Aristotle resists as moral virtue or moral excellence (LAMBRECHT 1995, 63). Here, Aristotle states that men have many impulses and desires each of which deserves consideration, but none of which ought to be permitted to be dominating. Thus, all of these impulses and desire, Aristotle notes are subject to being controlled. Moral virtue comes into play in this regard e.g. courage will mediate between cowardice and rashness; liberality will bring a medium between stinginess and prodigality, etc. Corresponding to the rational part of human nature which is the type of excellence called intellectual virtue (LAMBRECHT 1995, 64), Aristotle says that man needs to organize, direct and control the affairs of his society.

In his view man, in combining his rational (Intellectual virtue) and moral virtue, remains the best of animals and unique in his nature. With this conception of human nature, Aristotle notes that man by nature is a political animal" [The Politics, BK1 ch.2, 1253^a4]. This means that man from birth has a strong inclination to live in a political community, interact with others, search for his needs; and exercise his political rights, freedom and power. This is due to man's unique nature characterized by two elements; (a) intellectual, and (b) moral life.

For Aristotle, man is a "political animal" due to his creative power, known as intellectual life. Aristotle sees that man by nature is gifted with certain potentials which can only be brought to actuality through an organized group where man can develop self-control, live in harmony with others and ensure that his needs are being achieved. By the virtue of being endowed with intellect, Aristotle notes that "man is the only animal who has been endowed with the gift of speech" [The Politics, Bk1 ch. 3, $1253^a a5$] here, Aristotle is of the opinion that only the human person is gifted with reason and is capable of developing a language as a medium of communication. For him, other lower animals are endowed with emotions or pains and these are non-rational beings. Boethius had once conceived of human person as "an individual substance of rational nature". Thus, in line with Aristotle's position, man by reason of his intellect is capable of organizing a political community, ruling others and in turn being ruled. Here, Aristotle suggests that man as a rational being has moral conscience. Man has his moral laws within him and he is an end unit to himself (OZUMBA 2000, 88).

Man as a political animal is also a moral being. In his words Aristotle states that "it is a characteristic of man that he alone has any sense of good and evil, of just and unjust and the like and the association of living beings who have in this sense make a family and state" [The Politics, Bk 1 ch.2, $1253^a 15$]. What Aristotle is saying here is that man in exercising his political ambition brings in the issue of morality as well. Aristotle here sees politics and morality as intermarried just like in the human nature; the individual is made up of body and soul, Aristotle sees further that man is a free being. Unlike Rousseau who believes that man is free but everywhere in chains freedom of man in Aristotle's view is backed up with action. Thus, he writes, "life is action and not production...."[The Politics, Bk 1. Ch11; $1245^a 5$]. Here the responsibility attached to human freedom, Aristotle, affirms that persons are gifted with different talents and duties to be perform.

This is why for Aristotle issues like slavery and martyr, superior and inferior, authority and subordinates etc., are normal designs of life, they are part and parcel of nature. In this sense to be a slave for instance is not evil since you are meant to be so; some are born to rule and others to be ruled; some men by nature are free and others slaves, and for that, slavery is both expedient and right [The Politics, Bk 1 ch5, 1255^a]. Again, in human nature, Aristotle says that the male is by nature superior, and the female is inferior. This principle of necessity extends to all mankind [The Politics, Bk 1. Ch.5, $1254^b10\text{-}15$]. What Aristotle is saying in essence is that freedom and individual responsibility must always go together. The fact that one is placed in a certain position does not make one so special or above others. The fact that you are a governor of state and the other a house cleaner does not make you a better person than the cleaner; it is rather the work of nature that you should be in one place and other persons in another place. And that is why in human nature; Aristotle suggests that every part is very important. In this regard, if there is no slavery, there is no master in the true sense, if there is no student there will be no teacher, if there are no subjects, it will be meaningless to talk of authority (sovereign) and so on. Therefore, the dual role in nature including that of human, Aristotle affirms is not a contradiction of nature but a matter of necessity and expedience, hence such a duality exists in living musical mode [The Politics, Bk 1 Ch 5:30].

Aristotle's Theory of the State
Aristotle's conception of what is the nature of a state follows from the reason that he has unique stand about human person who is capable of managing the affairs of the state. This led him to postulate that both the individual person and the state has a natural cause of origin. And that the human person with his natural endowments is capable of living in an organized group which Aristotle calls a political community (state).

In his political theory of the state, Aristotle recognizes the fact that politic must be exercised in an organized group such as a state and that it is expedient for the individual's well-being. With this conception, Aristotle affirms that the individual by nature is destined to live in a state and the state like every other community is "established with a view to accomplish some good", or exists for some end. For Aristotle, the family exists primarily to preserve life. The state comes into existence in the first instance to preserve life for families and villages, which in the long run are not self-sufficing. Thus, when several villages are united into a single complete community, large to be nearly or quite self-sufficing, the state comes into existence, originating in the bare needs for life, and continuing in existence for the sake of a good life [The Politics, Bk1, ch 2, 1252^a25].

The origin of the state of Aristotle is a natural one prior to the family and to the individual, and the individual when isolated, is not self-sufficiency. And therefore he is like part in relation to the whole [The Politics, Bk1 ch.2, 1253^a25]. Both the state and the individual person, is endowed by nature with a distinctive function combining these two ideas, Aristotle says that "it is evident that the state is a creature of nature, and that man is by nature a political animal" [The Politics, Bk 1. Ch. 2, 1253^a]. So closely does Aristotle relate the individual and the state as to conclude that "he who is unable to live in society, or who has no need because he is sufficient for himself, must be either a beast or a god". Here, Aristotle has shown beyond reasonable doubt that the individual must live in a group, what he calls political community (state). The state through her leaders must ensure that the individual needs are provided. Thus, he writes: Every state is a community of some kind, and every community is established with a view to some good; for mankind always acts in order to obtain that which they think good. But, if all communities aim at some good, the state or political community which is the highest of all, and which embraces all the rest, aims at good in a greater degree than any other, and at the highest good [The Politics, BKI, Ch. I, 1252^a].

Aristotle went further to assert that in order to ensure healthy living among individuals, the state must ensure that its primary duty is that of formation and training of her members. Aristotle believes that apart from economic needs of the state, intellectual and moral education are paramount for good citizenship. In his Ethics Aristotle states clearly that "A state exists for the sake of a good life, and not for the sake of life only" [Nicomachean Ethics, B,K VII, Ch. 15 1334a 11]. What Aristotle is saying in essence is that a state would degenerate even in economic progression if the members of that state are not morally or intellectually sound. The cause of economic degeneration of a given state becomes high in the absence of moral conducts and intellectual performance. "Education", for Aristotle, "must follow the natural order of human development beginning with the body, dealing next with the appetites and training, the intellect last of all". Therefore, for a state to worth its name, there are certain conditions that must be met. But in all of these conditions such as economic needs, the virtues of moral and intellectual living are the most important. Aristotle writes: "It is clear then that a state is not a mere society, having a common place, established for the prevention of mutual crime and for the sake of exchange. These are conditions without which a state cannot exist, but all of them together do not constitute a state, which is a community of families in well-being, for the sake of a perfect and self sufficing. The end of the state is the good life and these are the means towards it. And the state is the union of families and villages in a perfect and self-sufficing life, by which we mean a happy an honorable life" [The Politics, Bk III, Ch. 9. 1280^b 30-40].

Aristotle, having stated clearly the responsibility of the state towards the individuals, set out in his project to state what should be the role of individuals within a political community as well, thus, he writes: "every political society exists for the sake of noble actions, and not of mere companionship. Hence, they who contribute more to such a society have the same or a greater freedom or nobility of birth but are inferior to them in Political virtue; or than those who exceed them in wealth but are surpassed by them in virtue" [The Politics, BK III Ch. 9, 1281^a5]. Here, Aristotle is of the opinion that each and every individual in the state must contribute his/her quota for the growth of the state through rendering services and labour force. Thus, what counts highest about an individual member of the state is virtue (Moral and intellectual life) than wealth or money. A person may have enough riches but when his conducts are bad (not morally sound) or is not highly intelligent or (not educated at all) and as such does not consider the well-being of the state such a person is an "inferior" member of that sate. Thus, for Aristotle "Virtue is more precious than gold". It means then that those who are qualified to lead the affairs of the state must be men of noble character, good and just. Thus, he writes; the rival claims of candidates for office (in a state) can only be based on the possession of elements which enter into the composition of a state. And therefore, the noble, or freeborn, or rich, may with good reason claim office; for holders of offices must be freemen and tax-payers; a state can be no more composed entirely of poor men than entirely of slaves. But if wealth and freedom are necessary elements, justice and valour are equally, so; for without the former qualities a state cannot exist at all, without the latter, not well [The Polities, Bk III Ch 12, 1283^a].

The question now raised is: How can we reconcile the autonomy of the individual person with the supremacy of the state? How would the individual's need in the state be evenly distributed by the state and the individual in turn ensure the healthy living of the state? On what grounds should we ensure the healthy living of the individual and state relationship? Is man for the state or the state for man? In tackling this problem further, we cannot dispute the fact that both the individual and the state must exist. Man is a being-with-other as Martin Heidegger rightly points out. Man is a being who is set towards the realization of his possibilities not as an isolated ego, but as a being that is necessarily interrelated with the world of things and world of persons. And because his self-sufficiency is so limited, man must band with his fellow men to supply his needs. Individuals and families are often obliged to subordinate their private good to the common good. In other instances individuals sometimes would be obliged to sacrifice their lives for the state, as in war, for the common good of all. The state in turn must not compromise man's natural right because they are given by a higher law. The state itself is but one of the means granted to man by the natural law to help him in achieving his last end (FAGOTHEY 1963, 325).

The state exists to protect life, liberty and property of all. By this very reason, the individual may be called long to play his part in the common defense even at the expense of his own life, liberty and property. With this conception, Aristotle has shown undoubtedly that the state is created for the good of man and for his harmonious existence. But on issue of evenly distributed or resources to individuals, Aristotle is of the opinion that in the state equals should be treated equally and unequal being treated unequally. This is the idea of social justice were everyone is to be given what is his/her due.

Recognizing the fact that a state emerged from a community, Aristotle States that a state could organize itself into at least any of the three kinds of government. The basic difference among them is primarily the number of rulers each has. A government can have as its ruler one, a few, or many. But each of these forms of government can have a true or a perverted form. When governments functions rightly, it governs for the common good of all the people; but a government is perverted when its rulers govern for their private gain or interest.

The true forms of each type of government, according to Aristotle are monarchy (one), aristocracy (few), and constitutional-government or polity (many). The perverted forms are; tyranny (one), oligarch (few) and democracy (many). [The Politics, BK III, Ch 6, 1279^b25]. Among these forms of government, Aristotle preferred aristocracy. This is because in aristocracy, there is the rule of a group of people whose degree of excellence, achievement, and ownership of property makes them responsible, able, and capable of command (STUMPF 1971, 104). Of the other forms of government in their perverted nature, Aristotle notes that "tyranny is a kind of monarchy which is for the interest of the monarch (ruler) only; oligarchy has in view the interest of the wealthy; democracy, of the needy; none of them discharge for the common good of all exception.

As discussed earlier on, Aristotle's concept of human nature is in two dimensions. The human person is made up of body and soul. While the former is emotive, the latter is intellectual. Both of them complement each other in the constitutive part of man. That is, the body and soul need each other. However, Aristotle recognizes the fact that the soul rules over the body, just like the intellect (reason) rules over the emotional part or passions.

Man also, in his intellectual and moral virtue shows the need for political community since he needs the other person for self-gratification or self-sufficiency. In the same way, Aristotle sees that the state and the individual need each other. Both the state and the individual person have natural cause of existence. But just like the soul rules over the body, the state through its authority rules over the members of the state.

Hence, it is based on this conception of the dual nature of man that made Aristotle to see the dual roles that will be equally displayed by the state and individuals alike. While the state provides the basic needs of man; man in turn must ensure that equity, justice and peace that give room for harmonious co-existence in a state are ensured. The individual members on their part must participate actively in running the affairs of the state.

Aristotle's conception of human nature is unique in the sense that man for him is a composite being. In his dual nature man is made up of body and soul; the soul is intellectual virtue and the body an emotional virtue. The former enables man to be rational and as such supersedes the rest of lower animals, while the latter is an irrational part which man shares with other animals. The rational part of man enables him to organize, direct and control the affairs of others. And it is only in the community (Political) that man finds his fulfillment through free interaction and sharing with others. However, most philosophers like Machiavelli conceives the irrational part of man as superseding the rational part but Aristotle believes that irrational part of man(emotion or passion) is subject to being controlled and that the rational parts of man (intellect) remains in control. Similarly, the state exists for this very purpose.

It is also similar with the individual parts which exist together, while the soul controls the activities of these bodily parts of man.

The state for Aristotle exists to care for man's needs (who must exist in a group with others). Thus, both man and the state have natural causes of existence. With this conception, the state, through her sovereign, rules over the members just like the soul rules over the body; yet both of them need the other in a complementary form. Man in his rational and moral virtue, is also a political animal by natural right or expediency. In a nutshell, Aristotle's political theory of the state and the human nature need commending.

CHAPTER FOURTEEN

PHILOSOPHY AFTER ARISTOTLE

Background

After the Socratic or Aristotelian period, we have a number of movements or schools that dominated the philosophical scene. Notable among these are the peripatetics, Epicureans, the cynics, the stoics, and the skeptics.

According to S. E. Stumpf, the flowering of these schools came on the heels of the decline of the Greek hegemony. The Roman Empire was at this time on the ascendancy and was fast assimilating other cultures and changing the events of history worldwide. The corresponding attitude at this time was that of independence. The intellectual, social, political and psychology mood was deeply affected. The corollary was a change in emphasis. Intellectuals (philosophers) became less interested in the communal existence of the city states which had crumbled at the end of the Peloponnesian war in which Athens was defeated and humbled.

The need of the hour was how individuals can lead meaningful lives. The concern at this time was "the person" and his well being. The quest for survival and having an attitude that will enhance fruitful, profitable and pleasurable life was the order. The old intellectual dispensation of contemplation and theorizing gave way to practical issues of life. Though these philosophies of this period are not completely novel in mood and emphasis, they differ from their pedigrees.

1. The Peripatetics

The peripatetics are the immediate successors of Aristotle represented by Theophrastus and Strato of Lampsacus. (OWENS 1959, 363). The period of the peripatetics is fixed around 370-285 BC. The account of the life of Theophrastus of Eresus in given by Diogenes Laertius. Eresus is on the Island of Lesbos very close to Assos.

Theophrastus is reported to have attended Plato's discourses and must have met Aristotle in Athens when he was still at Plato's Academy. It is said that a close intimacy developed between him and Aristotle. Theophrastus whose original name was Tyrtamus became a disciple of Aristotle. It was Aristotle who changed his name from Tyrtamus to Theophrastus because of his gift of eloquence (OWENS 1959, 363). He took over Aristotle's Lyceum when he left for Chalcis and is said to have acquired the possession of Aristotle's library.

Very little is known about the Peripatetics as no fragments of their wittings remain extant. Our mention of them is simply to maintain a historical order and to put in chronological perspective the direction of philosophical works after Aristotle.

2. Epicurus

Epicurus was born eight years after Plato's death and Aristotle was about forty two years old (STUMPF 1971, 115). Epicurus was born in 342 BC on the Island of Samos. He was influenced by the atomistic philosophy of Democritus. Epicurus was concerned with finding a principle for living. He is called a practical philosopher who saw "philosophy as the medicine of the soul".

In his moral doctrines, he posited that the chief aim of human life is pleasure. The standard of goodness is pleasure. Pleasure for him should be the chief end of all human endeavor. Epicurus noted and emphasized that not all, pleasures are good. The guiding principle is to minimize pain. Any pleasure therefore which will produce more pain is not worth the effort. He drew a hierarchy of pleasure. At the apex are intellectual pleasures which give mental balance and satisfaction with minimum pain. The other pleasures are fleeting pleasures like seeking for fame, sensual satisfaction, popularity, wealth, etc., these are not as good as the former because the more of these pleasures we attain the more insatiable we find ourselves. Epicurus did not explicate in detail how we can derive pleasure that is completely devoid of pain.

He is quoted as saying that "pleasure is the first good innate in us and from pleasure we begin every act of choice and avoidance and to pleasure we return again" (STUMPF 1971, 118). Feeling and sensation are like thermometers which we use to ascertain whether an action is pleasurable or not. It is his emphasis on feeling and sensation that has led to the misinterpretation of his moral theory as permissive and promotive of all kinds of illicit pleasure. For him, pleasure does not consist in profligacy, eating, drinking, sex and reveling because at the end of those comes intense pain. That kind of pleasure is therefore not worth the resulting pain. We are to avoid such pleasures which entail continuous indulgence.

He is also remembered for his atomistic philosophy. Like Democritus, he said that atoms are the basic constituent of all things. This means that only atoms are eternal. For him, there is no God the creator but atom began to exist from the beginning. This means that at death what happens is that the constituent atoms disintegrate into atoms which return to the pool of other atoms from where cosmic processes are generated. The truth is that there exists a God who is the creator of all things, is interested and involved in human affairs. This view of Epicurus is only to be received with a pinch of salt. However, consideration must be given to the limited religious light which he received at the time of his philosophizing.

3. Stoicism

Stoicism as a school of philosophy was founded by Zeno in 334BC. He established his school on the *Stoa or porch*. Many scholars were attracted to his school. Notable among them are Cleanthes and Aristo. Others who were later inspired by Zeno's thought include Cicero, Epictetus, Seneca, and the Emperor Marcus Aurelius. All these came between 4th BC to 180 AD.

The courageous death of Socrates acted as a fillip to the philosophical disposition of Zeno. He discerned a lot of moral virtue in the life and principles of Socrates. The need to confront evil and adversities of life with boldness is a very worthy lesson he learned from Socrates.

The Stoics aimed at happiness but did not expect like Epicurus to derive it from pleasure. They rather sought for happiness through wisdom. Their view is that since we cannot control events, we can control our attitude towards the events. It is like the popular sayings that "if you cannot control the inevitable, then, cooperate with it".

It is useless to fear future events. We must, like, Socrates with serenity; boldness and courage face death and other challenging events of life. For the stoics, there is a principle of purpose infused in nature. This is the principle of Reason and law. God for them is a rational being who orders all things according to divine purpose. This means that whatever happens must necessarily happen and there is a purpose for it. It is likely to work out a divine purpose. Men are enjoined not to resist events but rather to adopt the attitude of "stoic indifference". It is a theory of equanimity of the soul and imperturbability of the spirit. It is the attitude of calm disposition and total resignation to divine free and natural events.

For the stoics, matter is the basis of all reality. They could not understand God as transcending matter. The material rational fire which steers all things they call God. Epictetus is quoted as saying "if I cannot escape death, can't I escape the dread of it? We are free to choose our attitude but not free to choose what happens to us. Though providence rules everything, it does not rule our attitudes. There is no contradiction here, because, it is God that conditions our capacity to be able to react this way or that way—which means, He is still ultimately in control. Reason is the common property of God and men. This makes it possible for all men to share in the reasonableness of God and to attest to the existence of universal law and justice. Men who act according to the true dictate of their conscience cannot do wrong but will walk in line with God's divine ordering of things.

The Stoics are important because they teach us the need to cooperate with the inevitable and to face the challenges of life with boldness.

4. The Cynics

The cynics originated between 410-320BC. Diogenes of Sinope is known as a leading figure of this school. Sinope is his birth place and is a colony of Miletus. He was later exiled and this took him to

Athens. He is said to be well known in Athens as the 'the dog' (Owen: 365). Much of what we know about him is received from Diogenes Laertius. He is said not to have left any writings. According to Owens, it is difficult to piece together with certainty any consistent philosophical doctrine that could be called the philosophy of the Cynics. Some even maintain that Cynicism is not a philosophy at all, but just a manner of living (OWENS 1959, 366). The Cynics tended to emphasize the need for a practical life that is oriented towards the teaching and practice of virtue.

'Cynic' means 'dog'. It is a contemptuous name given to them for their attitude of isolationism, self sufficiency and separatism. In Homeric usage the word cynic, carries the import of 'shamelessness'. It is said that Diogenes (their leader) and his disciples lived like dogs. The cynics themselves inverted the meaning and rather saw themselves as the true watch dogs of true philosophic wisdom and virtue.

Diogenes Laertius noted that the statue of Diogenes bore the epithet "thou alone didst point out on mortals the lesson of self-sufficiency and the easiest path of life" (OWENS 1959, 366). Diogenes of Sinope is said to have thought the doctrine of self *sufficing-ness* or separateness of existence. They had their attitude of disdaining the superfluities and austerity and asceticism as the path to peace and happiness. They were against conventions and sought to live as simply and bare as they could. It was life devoid of ostentations. Their motto is "change the currency", that is, a critical and repulsive attitude to conventions and vogues. They rejected the norms of Greek social life. Diogenes of Sinope saw himself as a cosmopolitan citizen with no nativity – He was a citizen of the world.

Diogenes of Sinope taught asceticism. For him, asceticism means living out of the fruit of diligence, hard work, and Spartan-like spirit, that is, hardy, undaunted and enduring. The cynics are trained to endure physical hardships, poverty, contempt, insult and the like. It also implies living in freedom from the restraints of life (OWENS 1959, 367). Man is therefore encouraged not to be entangled in the affairs of riches which may rob him of serenity of mind.

The cynics have a lot to teach us especially in the face of present day craze for materialism and pleasure seeking. To be happy, we must be content with such things we have. It was Jesus who said that "a man's life does not consist in the abundance of the things he possesses (LUKE 12 verse 15). It is a worthy lesson for us today and for this the cynics will ever be remembered.

5. Skepticism

Skepticism is derived from the word skeptic which in turn comes from the Greek word *skeptesthai,* which means to look carefully at, to examine and consider. The skeptics were later known as *Aporetics* and *Ephetics* because of their deliberate habit of suspending judgment. They carried out *epode*, disinclination, suspension of judgment and remained in the state of *aporia* that is, not having any firm opinion on any thing. They were also called Zetetics which means seekers because they were always seeking to know the truth.

We had two traditional types of skepticism, each hostile to the other. But, both converged in the skepticism of Aenesidemus (OWENS 1959, 368). The older traditional is called pyrrhonism and the later is called Academic skepticism. The Academic version of skepticism flourished in Plato's Academy. Much of what we know about skepticism came from Diogenes Laertius, Cicero and Sextus Empiricus who himself was the last of Pyrrhonist writer. Notable skeptics include Pyrrho of Elis, Timon his pupil Arcecilaus, Carneades, Gorgias of Leontini, Aenesidemus, Cicero, Sextus Empiricus and others.

Pyrrho the founder of skepticism lived between 365 and 275BC. He was first a painter before he under-took the pursuit of philosophy. Pyrrho is said to enunciate the philosophy of maintaining that virtue was the only good. He was known to have lived piously. He thought that we never can be sure of the truth, everything is indifferent. Nothing abides, or is fixed, rather, it is appearance and custom that fixes the way things are. The way things are do not provide the possibility of stating definitely that a thing is either this way or that way.

Owens quotes him (Pyrrho) as saying that "there is not a single thing about which one can say 'it is' rather than 'it is not', or 'it both is and is not' 'or it neither is nor is not'". This means that a thing is no more this than that. This means that things are uncertain, indeterminate and imprecise. This enjoins all to remain without inclining to any opinion. This means abstaining from judgment of truth or falsity. This is accompanied by the disposition of *epoche;* that is suspension of judgment and the result is what they call the state of ataraxia or unpertubedness of mind. To have peace of mind never be steadfast in the asserting of any opinion. This theory of Pyrrho and his disciple Timon of Philus is a form of agnosticism, that is, "I don't knowism".

As Timon is quoted as saying "Things are by nature indifferent. We have nothing to express about them, and the reward is *ataraxy*. "Appearance and the customary prevail everywhere".

Academic Skepticism

Apart from Pyrrhonism, we have what we call Academic skepticism we have about five Academies. The first is that of Plato and his immediate successors, the second or middle Academy is dominated by Arcesilaus and his group. The third Academy is spearheaded by Carneades of Cyrene and his successor Clitomachus of Carthage. According to Sextus Empiricus some writers add a fourth and fifth Academies headed by Philo of Larissa and Antichus of Ascalon respectively.

Arcesilaus one of the founders of the Academic school held an extreme view. For him, there is nothing that can be known. He says that equally strong reason can be provided for both sides of contradictory positions. A wise man should withhold decisive assent on any issue because we never can be sure which assertion is true or false. This is similar to Gorgias' position, that (1) Nothing exist (2) if anything exist, it cannot be known (3) if it can be known, it cannot be communicated.

Gorgias was an extreme skeptic who drove the skeptical doubt and uncertainty to its extreme negative limits. For Carneades, there is extremely no criterion of truth. There is no way of distinguishing a true appearance from a false appearance. The best one can be sure of is probability and we must be content with it in its various degrees (Owens: 373).

Later, Greek skepticism was continued by Aenesidenus of Crete. He talks about the fact that nothing can be proved with finality, thus highlighting the problem of infinite regress. He mentioned the relativity of perceptions, the impossibility of establishing satisfactory hypothesis, the problem of circularity, that human cognitive process is unreliable and the fact that causality is unintelligible, imperceptible and unclear.

From the foregoing it is clear that the skeptics are all agreed that we cannot have certain knowledge and that judgment about truth and falsity cannot be settled with finality and that we cannot differentiate appearance from reality in any clear-cut way. This means that absolute knowledge is impossible. Only knowledge of appearance can be possible. The question is, how can we achieve certain knowledge in the realm of philosophy if the position of skepticism is true? This is the crux of the matter which epistemology (theory of knowledge) as a branch of philosophy treats. It does appear that for us to achieve certain knowledge, the challenge of the skeptics must be tackled. Skepticism can only be overcome if we accept that philosophical knowledge should be limited to the probable, uncertain and relative.

Relevant Literature

1. ALLEN, Reginald. [Greek Philosophy: Thales to Aristotle], 1966. The Fress Press: New York. Paperback.

2. ARISTOTLE. [Ethics], Transl. by J. A. K. Thomson,1976. Penguin Books: London. Paperback.

3. ___ . [The Politics], 1962. Penguin Books: London. Paperback.

4. ___ . [The Politics], Trans. Mortimer J. Adler, 1993. Oxford University Press: London. Paperback.

5. ___ . [On the Soul] (De anima), Trans. Mortimer J. Adler, 1993. Oxford University Press: London. Paperback.

6. ___ . [Nicomachean Ethics], Trans. Mortimer J. Adler, 1993. Oxford University Press: London. Paperback.

7. BECKMAN, James. [The Religious Dimensions of Socrates' Thought],1999. Wilfred Laurier University Press. Paperback.

8. COPLESTON, Fredrick. [A History of Philosophy], 1967. Image Books: New York. Paperback.

9. CORNFORD, F. M. [Plato's Theory of Knowledge], 1979. Routledge and Kegan Paul: London. Paperback.

10. DURANT, Will. [The Story of Philosophy: The Lives and Opinions of the World Greatest Philosophers, from Plato to Dewey],1995. New York, Paperback.

11. FAGOTHEY, Austin. [Right and Reason], 1963. The C.V. Mosby Company: London. Paperback.

12. GUTHRIE, M. A. [History of Greek Philosophy], Vol.1, 1978. Cambridge University Press: London. Paperback.

13. HAMILTON, Edith and Huntington Cairns eds. [The Collected Dialogues of Plato], 1961. Princeton University Press: New Jersey. Paperback.

14. LAMBRECHT, S. [Our Philosophical Tradition: A Brief History of Western Civilization], 1995. Appleton-Century-croft, Inc.: New York.

15. JONES, W. T. [The Classical Mind; A History of Western Philosophy], 2nd edition, 1970. Harcourt Brace Jovanovich Publishers: New York. Paperback.

16. LEWES, G. J. A. [A Biographical History of Philosophy], 1957. W. Parker and Sons: London. Paperback.

17. MAUTNER, Thomas, ed. [The Penguin Dictionary of Philosophy], 1996. Penguin Books: London. Paperback.

18. OWENS, Joseph. [A History of Ancient Western Philosophy], 1959. Prentice Hall, Inc.,: New Jersey. Paperback.

19. OZUMBA, Godfrey. [A Concise Introduction to Epistemology], 2001. Ebenezer Computer Service: Calabar. Paperback.

20. ___. and Jonathan CHIMAKONAM. [Njikoka Amaka: Further Discussions on the Philosophy of Integrative Humanism], 2014. 3rd Logic Option Publishing: London. Paperback.

21. ___. [The Great Philosophers] Vol.III, 2000. R & K Publishers: Awka. Paperback.

22. ___. [The Great Philosophers], Vol.1 1996. Cantaur Press: Calabar. Paperback.

23. ___. [A Course Text on Ethics], 2001. O.O.P Limited: Lagos. Paperback.

24. PLATO. [The Republic], 5th Edition, Trans. Stumpf. E., 1971. McGraw Hill: New York. Paperback.

25. ___. [Protagoras], 1956. Bobbs-Marill Company: New York. Paperback.

26. RUSSELL, Bertrand. [History of Western Philosophy], 1945. George Allen and Univ. in Ltd.,: London. Paperback.

27. STUMPF, Enoch. [Philosophy, History and Problem], 1971. McGraw Hill: New York. Paperback.

28. UDUIGWOMEN, Andrew, ed. [Metaphysics: A Book of Readings], 2012. Ultimate Index Publishers: Calabar. Paperback.

29. ___. and Ozumba, G. O. [A Concise Introduction to Philosophy and Logic], 2000. Centaur Publishers: Calabar. Paperback.

30. WERNER, Jaeger. [Aristotle: Fundamentals of the History of His Development], 1962. Oxford University Press: London. Paperback.

Index

A
Academy, 74, 82, 121.
Achilles, 37.
Air, 20-21, 24, 26, 29, 34, 41-42, 46, 48, 52, 94-95.
Alexander the Great, 88.
Anaximander, 5, 7, 13-21, 31, 52.
Anaximenes, 5, 7, 19-21, 24, 26, 52.
Andronicus of Rhodes, 89, 94.
Anselem, 47.
Anthropomorphic, 23.
Apeiron, 17.
Aquinas Thomas, 126.
Aristocracy, 86, 112.
Aristotle, 4, 88-116.
Asia Minor, 7, 126.
Atomism, 10, 12, 47, 50, 52-53.

C
Categories, 89-90, 93, 101.
Chimakonam Jonathan, 59, 124.
Cicero, 89, 120.
Copleston, Fredrick, 3, 9, 47, 53, 58, 99.
Cosmogony, 1.
Cosmology, 31, 64.

D
Democracy, 55, 65, 69, 82, 85-86, 92, 112.
Democritus, 47-51, 97.
Dialectics, 35, 58, 60, 73, 77, 80, 86, 93.
Dialogues, 71-72, 81, 83, 93.

Diogenes, Laertius, 9, 47, 119-120.

E
Earth, 8, 14, 20-21, 23-24, 34, 41-42, 48-49, 100.
Egypt, 31.
Eleatics, 39, 62.
Empedocles, 40-42, 44, 46, 48-49, 60, 62.
Epicureans, 4, 115.
Epicurus, 47-48, 116-117.
Eristics, 65.

F
Fire, 18, 24-27, 34, 48, 118.
Flux, 24-25, 58, 62, 83.

G
God-gods, 1-2, 10, 23, 50, 58, 64-65, 79, 81, 90-91, 109, 117-118.
Golden Era, 4, 67-68, 79, 82, 88.
Gorgias of Leontini, 60, 62-64, 66, 83, 121-122.
Greek, 1, 4, 83, 115, 122.

H
Haley's river, 10-11.
Hedonism, 4.
Hellenistic, 3-4.
Heraclitus, 7, 24-28, 35, 52, 58, 62, 82-83.
Homeric-Homer, 23, 64, 79, 119.

I
Ionia, 4, 23.
Jones, W. T., 20-21.

L
Leibniz, G. W., 10-12.
Leucippus, 47.
Logos, 25-26.
Lucretius, 47.
Lyceum, 88, 116.

M
Mautner, Thomas, 92-93, 97.
Melissus, 60.
Metaphysics, 5, 22, 83-84, 90-97, 103.
Miletus, 5, 19, 47, 118.
Motion, 8-9, 41, 43, 49, 90, 94.
Myths, 1-2, 6.

N
Nicomachean, 93, 110.
Nicomachean ethics, 93, 110.
Nous, 42, 45-47, 49.

O
Oligarchy, 92, 112.
Owens, Joseph, 7, 119, 121-122.

P
Paradox, 6, 35, 37.
Parmenides, 27-30, 49, 58, 62, 83.
Pericles-Periclean, 43, 82.
Plato, 4, 53, 67, 75, 82-88, 99, 104, 121.
Plotinus, 4.

Pluralism, 36, 46.
Pyrrho- pyrrhonism, 120-121.
Pythagoras, 10, 12, 25, 30-33, 35, 37, 49.

R
Roman, 3-4, 115.

S
Sextus Empiricus, 60, 120-121.
Skepticism, 23, 56, 60, 66, 120-121.
Skeptics, 4, 83, 115, 120, 122.
Socrates, 4, 65-79, 80-88, 90, 97, 101, 117-118.
Sophism, 55-56, 64.
Sophists, 54, 65, 69, 71, 77, 79, 80, 83, 85.
Soul, 8-10, 118, 113.
Stoicism, 4, 117.
Stoics, 4, 117-118.
Stumpf, Enoch, 10, 115-117.
Syllogism, 28, 90, 101, 103.

T
Thales of Miletus, 1, 8-15, 17, 20, 24, 29, 49, 52.
Theogony, 1.
Theology, 2.
Thrasymachus, 59, 64-65.
Tortoise, 37.

U
Unity, 9, 17, 21, 27, 29, 39, 41, 52, 98.

V
Vitalism, 10, 11.

W
Water, 8-12, 13, 15-18, 25-26, 41, 49, 52, 102.

X
Xenophanes, 23, 60.

Z
Zeno, 35-36, 38, 40, 47, 60, 117.
Zeus, 2, 23.

www.ingramcontent.com/pod-product-compliance
Lightning Source LLC
Chambersburg PA
CBHW032037040426
42449CB00007B/924